SECOND CHANCE
Women Returning to Study

Joan E. Martin

Penguin Books

Penguin Books Australia Ltd.,
487 Maroondah Highway, P.O. Box 257
Ringwood, Victoria 3134, Australia
Penguin Books Ltd,
Harmondsworth, Middlesex, England
Viking Penguin Inc,
40 West 23rd Street, New York, N.Y. 10010, U.S.A.
Penguin Books Canada Limited,
2801 John Street, Markham, Ontario, Canada L3R 1B4
Penguin Books (N.Z.) Ltd,
182-190 Wairau Road, Auckland 10, New Zealand

First published by Penguin Books Australia, 1988

Copyright © Joan E. Martin, 1988

Typeset in Palatino 9½/12 by Allset Graphics
Made & printed in Australia by The Book Printer

Martin, Joan E.

Bibliography.
Includes index.
ISBN 0 14 010584 0.

1. Higher education of women — Australia.
2. Women — Education — Australia. I.
Title.

376′.65′0994

Penguin Books
SECOND CHANCE

Joan Martin was born in Rockhampton in 1934 and lived
in Brisbane until 1955 when she married and moved
to Sydney. When the youngest of her three children
was nine months old she began studying for HSC by
correspondence.

After training as a teacher she moved to Melbourne in
1967. Since then, while continuing to teach, she has
completed an Honours Arts degree, a Master of Education
and, in 1986 was awarded a PhD for her research in the
area of mature age women as students.

For my mother, who felt but did not understand her gentle oppression.

CONTENTS

ACKNOWLEDGEMENTS

In the years that I have been researching and writing on women returning to study I have been assisted by many people in many different ways, but it is impossible to list them all.

To the women who participated in the research, I owe a debt, not only because they gave me their time, but also because they allowed me to share with them many of their personal experiences as mature-age students and as family members. The personnel in the women's learning centres, Council of Adult Education centres and high-school evening schools which I visited were also very helpful, and I wish to thank them.

To Dr Shirley Sampson, who supervised my PhD research, I give my sincere thanks. She offered her intellectual and moral support wholeheartedly and her experience and guidance were invaluable.

I am grateful to all the friends, family members and fellow research students with whom I discussed various aspects of my work. Two friends of very long standing, Jean Cooper and Margaret Malone, gave me constructive criticism and unwavering support. I do thank them for their faith in my ability to succeed.

I had always hoped that what I was discovering could be passed on to other adult students and educators, but my work might have remained on academic shelves only had it not been for the insight of Barbara Burton at Penguin. Her enthusiasm and encouragement in the task of turning my thesis into a readable book is very much appreciated. I have great respect for Venetia Nelson, my editor, who has made the reshaping of my research finding into this book yet another valuable learning experience for me. Thank you.

INTRODUCTION

When I returned to study, I did not step outside the door of my Sydney home except, of course, to check the letterbox for that large envelope which provided the link between me, a wife and mother at home with three small children, and the outside world of ideas, action and interesting people. The regular communications with my correspondence tutors were like love letters in that they swept me into a whirl of anticipation and excitement. I knew not the reason for this exhilaration, nor did I question it. It was enough to relish the realisation that I shared the products of my mind, both in humanities and in mathematics, with people who recognised my strengths and patiently pointed out my weaknesses. They knew nothing of my personal life, except perhaps that I bore the title 'Mrs'.

I pursued those five subjects with all the appetite and energy of a hungry Oliver, and always I wanted more—more books to read, more comments from my unseen mentors, more time. Ah, time! It played tricks with me, tricks that always ended in my feeling guilty.

★ The baby is asleep. Hope he sleeps until I finish this essay. I shouldn't wish for that. I should be enjoying him while the others are at school. I do. I do, but not *all* the time. God, I feel guilty. Why aren't I satisfied with this pleasant home and great family? Why? Don't know. Stop thinking about it. What *do* I think of 'The Superannuated Man' by Charles Lamb?

All that was a generation ago. The 22 years have been filled with child-rearing, marriage, study, working part-time and full-time and growing older—growing older, but not necessarily wiser. The steps or stages have been negotiated simply because they presented themselves. One thing led to another, as they say. There was so much to do in my double life, for that is how it ran: along parallel tracks which rarely met, and then only in times of upheaval. When a train hits something head on, the rails generally buckle and cross. My task was to ensure that there were no such confrontations.

The research which I undertook for a PhD began out of a genuine desire to understand what had become by the middle to late 1970s a phenomenon in education: the return to study of thousands of mature-age women. Observing the large numbers of women who were studying for the Higher School Certificate (now the Victorian Certificate of Education) and other bridging and preparatory programs, and who were entering colleges and universities, I began to realise that I had been a pioneer. When I taught a group of women at a high-school evening class, this feeling was reinforced, and I felt a genuine empathy with them and even understood some of their unspoken tensions. I knew, or thought I knew, that education was a great liberator of women. One had only to witness the numbers with degrees and diplomas who were now earning a living as teachers, social workers and librarians while at the same time contributing substantially to the family income. It had not really occurred to me to question why we subject ourselves to hours of work, go to extraordinary lengths to meet deadlines, bend over backwards to meet family commitments, and underscore all this physical and mental effort with the leaden emotion of guilt. There was a tremendous sense of achievement at having reached each stage on the educational ladder and that was enough to keep me going.

Only now am I able to look back on my own development and see the driving forces, the inhibiting factors, the wrong turns and the right ones; but this is not because my persistent pursuit of academic credentials made me wise—quite the opposite. I realise my folly. What has happened is this: in the process of my research, 146 women over the age of 25 who live in metropolitan Melbourne volunteered to complete a questionnaire giving details of their personal experiences and aspirations as adult students. Forty-six of these women offered to meet me personally and to discuss their experiences in more detail. Each of the women who contributed in this way provided another clue, another sometimes obscure piece in the jigsaw which illustrates the adult women learner in her social, economic and cultural environment. They shared their experiences with me and in so doing broke down the isolation which for so many years had acted as a smokescreen between me, the adult student, mother and worker, and the wider society.

I realised that there was an important distinction between education and learning. Education can be a package. It can be given subject labels and delivered like a commodity that we buy. We choose subjects out of interest, the need to gain a credential to re-enter the workforce, or because they are available at a time that fits into our busy timetable. Depending on the circumstances, we have the time to treat the subject in depth, or we feel plagued by the knowledge that we are skimming the surface. There are so many domestic and family demands. Occasionally we relate what we are learning to our own society and our position within it, but more often we take a fairly detached view of the knowledge we are acquiring. It is interesting and we certainly acquire more understanding of facts and events which have shaped the world. Of course, learning does take place when we are being educated. However, there is a risk that it will never be related to oneself, that is, that it will never be personalised. There is satisfaction in knowing more about the world, and this brings a degree of confidence, but often there is little improved understanding of ourselves or the positions we occupy in society. Learning that is liberating for the individual requires a determination to involve yourself through your experiences of life in the problems, issues and circumstances to which you are being introduced in your studies. The subject matter of the humanities and pure sciences are rich in human experiences which can serve to enhance our understanding of ourselves. Many of our assumptions about our abilities and our limitations as individuals can be challenged if we use education for learning. Some people make the connections between the subject matter of their studies and their own situations without much prompting. Others require the skills of a teacher to link their life experiences to historical and social issues.

In discussions with many many women, I found recurring problems and assumptions with which I identified. It was like *déjà vu,* but I had an urgent need to distance myself for fear of becoming too subjective in the approach to both the method for my research and the interpretation of the findings. For this reason, I deliberately tried to take myself *out* of the situation, although it is a very rare, perhaps non-existent researcher who can do this completely. It would be untruthful to claim that my own experiences had no bearing on the direction of the research, but one of the purposes of doing it was to weigh any of my own insights against a wider, more comprehensive body of observation, both theoretical and empirical, in order to arrive at a more balanced, less subjective understanding of the phenomenon. I wanted the responses of a large number of women of all ages and from all walks of life who were studying at all levels from preparatory classes to university degree courses, because I knew that we all faced similar problems. The possibilities were endless but the realities were limiting. Finance, time and the difficulty of handling large quantities of data by myself meant that I had to be satisfied with a fairly small sample. However, these women were sufficiently diverse in their social backgrounds, ages, expectations of study and types of courses being undertaken to allay any fear of the sample being unrepresentative. In fact it correlated very well with data I was able to gather on mature-age students doing secondary and tertiary studies in Australia.

I have jumped too quickly ahead. First, there was reading around the subject, then the development of a theoretical framework in which to develop the method and to interpret the findings. In social science research where data is drawn from individual and generally unrepeatable human experiences, there are no black-and-white findings. It does help in interpreting and analysing these human experiences to use a theoretical framework as a sounding board. The data can prove, disprove or modify the theory. I became critically aware of theories and texts on education and social change and, perhaps most importantly, I became aware of many of my own biases and perspectives. The theory which underlies my analysis of the data is one that is based on empirical research and has been the subject of much debate and discussion for some years. Broadly, it claims that formal education is effective in maintaining the social and cultural status quo, that is, in ensuring that the hierarchy of social relations continues, despite programs for the education of the masses, or, in this case, despite the educational attainments of adult women. As I mentioned previously, I began the research firm in the belief that a small but significant revolution was under way as more and more women took up their books and biros. A theory that suggested otherwise was a challenge to my perception of adult women returning to study. I had thought that social institutions, like marriage and family, would have been greatly affected by women taking an important step for themselves. Certainly I thought the workforce would be altered considerably by the numbers of newly educated women entering it.

When reading and analysing the answers to the questionnaires, it became obvious that elements were present which could not be ignored. For example, for over half of the respondents, a desire to return to work had *not* been a motivating factor. Expectations such as self-fulfilment, personal satisfaction and improved confidence raised questions about the self-image of women who felt the need to become students again. Additional information and comments, often written in the margins of the questionnaire sheets, or on additional pages, referred to two major concerns, among many other more minor ones: the attitudes of husbands, children and friends and the perception of the role of housewife as an extremely low-status one. That being a student is seen to be superior in status is illustrated by the following comment, which is one of many in this vein:

★ I never ever described myself as a housewife. Since I've started studying I feel much better about myself because there is something at the end.

Following another period of intensive reading, I began to understand some of the problems of adult women students in terms of what society expects of them, and what they assume about their own abilities and responsibilities. I could see that these factors influenced their reasons for seeking further education and often tempered or confused their expectations of it. For example, in our society most women are expected to accept prime responsibility for household management, although this activity rates very poorly in occupational status. When they become absorbed in an activity which will improve their status, a conflict arises between their own needs and those of the family. Another example of assumptions at government level is the imposition of administration fees for tertiary students. This is an action that rests on the assumption that students either have independent means or are able to pursue part-time work to earn money. *Not* addressed is the situation of many adult married women. If they have the skills to find part-time work, and if it is available, they then have to find the time to add paid work to their busy agenda which generally has as its top time priority almost total responsibility for household chores and child-rearing. Again, financial assistance, such as Austudy, is available only to full-time students.

If such attitudes and actions are to change, how will this come about? How and under what circumstances do people challenge or change their *own* assumptions? These questions became the basis for more reading and consideration in the context of adult education. I do not mean to elaborate on these theories here, but, for those who are interested, I do so in chapter 1 of my PhD thesis which is held at Monash University, Melbourne. I found that some assumptions are very deeply entrenched and have a profound effect on how the adult woman views her action in returning to study. If Guilt lurks, waiting to attack the unwary student who is torn between finishing an essay and attending to her family's needs, he generally manages to sap considerable energy, not to mention concentration, from his victim. I discuss this particular emotion and its attendant assumptions at some length in chapter 3. Personal time, social life, time spent with children, all suffer some modification in most cases. Attitudes to seeking a place in the workforce are also interesting.

I confessed earlier that I realise my folly. I can expand that statement a little to explain that I now understand the assumptions about society and my place in it which drove me on willy-nilly to seek academic credentials. Had I recognised these earlier, I would almost certainly have taken another path. The irony is, however, that the sharing of experiences with the women I encountered in the course of my research was the means by which this personal understanding developed. In other words, if I had not pursued this research for a PhD, the unique opportunity to learn through sharing of experiences would not have arisen. This is not to say that such learning environments where personal experiences are shared, discussed and analysed are not available, but they are sometimes unknown or inaccessible to returning students. There is also the fear of the unknown. For some, education belongs in a traditional classroom and credentials are the measure of success or otherwise.

The main purpose in writing this book on the basis of my research findings is to reach those mature-age women who have returned to study, or who are preparing to do so, regardless of whether they are studying Year 12 subjects or returning to do a higher degree. It would be wonderful if their family and friends could read it also. Some tensions might be recognised and even relieved. It is very important that I 'report back' to the interviewees and questionnaire respondents who contributed so willingly to my research. I am deeply grateful to them. For most, the experience was exhilarating. For others, it was very difficult, but as one woman said,

★ The benefits I have gained have far outweighed other considerations. In fact, I suspect that these very difficulties have been a determining factor in my growth. I feel a great personal freedom, due in part to my study.

I feel there is something to say to those who provide education for adults, particularly women, although I have come to see many parallels between the way they often see themselves in the social hierarchy and the position of unemployed, retrenched and early retired people also. In the following chapters I will reveal what I found about reasons for returning to study and what happens when you do. I will point to the joys and the limitations. By the final chapter, I hope the implications of these findings will clarify my statement about my folly, and raise some questions in the minds of my readers about their own assumptions.

PART 1
WHY RETURN TO STUDY?

ONE
REASONS — SPOKEN AND UNSPOKEN

★ I feel I am just an unpaid housekeeper, but when I study I can say, 'This is what I do'. (Betty, 32)

★ I hate writing 'secretary' because that doesn't tell people what I am. 'Secretary' puts me in a pigeonhole that I don't like. (Lorna, 37)

To isolate one factor as the sole motivation for an action is impossible, given the plethora of psychological, historical, social, political and economic forces which drive us. We each respond very differently to situations, depending, perhaps, on our expectations. The woman who has expected that marriage and having children will satisfy her completely may throw herself into that role, and never feel the need to change that image of self. She is lucky in a way, especially if she remains untouched by economic pressure to find a job. There has to be another ingredient for her contentment to be complete. The members of her family and social circle must provide sufficient affirmation of her role as wife and mother to maintain her positive view of self—her sense of self-worth. The self-description 'just a housewife' would never occur to her, because she would be safe in her family and social cocoon, free from niggling self-doubt. Who am I? What am I? These questions, often considered but rarely given voice, would either not be asked or would be answered confidently, without the slightest hint of defensiveness. If any doubt crept into a quiet conversation with self, then the happy housewife and mother would be reacting to some pressure from outside her circle. She might defend her position, in her own mind, or she might begin to feel the need to explore other means by which she could more confidently define her self.

External pressures subtly influence women to measure themselves against criteria by which the world outside the home assesses worth. Rarely are they ascribed status in their own right. A women's socioeconomic status is measured by the occupation of her husband, or, if she lives alone and/or supports a family, she has her individual status, but only very occasionally does she enter the higher echelons of society. First, women still earn less than men. The average weekly total earnings of full-time female employees is $393.20 compared with $498.20 for males. Second, even if a woman is highly qualified, she is usually ascribed a status below that of the male in a similar occupation. So what I am saying is this: unless a woman has either never asked the question 'Who am I?', or has asked it and received a reply completely devoid of defensiveness, she will act in some way to develop an acceptable self-image. For some, it will be Cordon Bleu cooking lessons. Cooking is creative and satisfying, provided, of course, one's efforts are appreciated. Voluntary work will absorb others. People feel good about doing something for those less fortunate than they are. Competitive sport is a popular outlet. Golf is perhaps the most individually testing, and there is some recognition of ability in winning or lowering a handicap.

We all need affirmation. That is true. What I have explored is the notion that adult education can supply this vital component in the building of a satisfactory self-image. I have questioned the assumption that education necessarily leads to an improved image of self. If it does, on what is this image built? On society's prescription of what you are worth as an educated person with a recognised credential, or on your own understanding of the forces in society, including education, which shape the self-image? I have found that some educational approaches have more capacity than others to achieve this understanding.

I dared not ask women in my sample the question 'Why did you return to study?' as I am well aware from my own experience of the defence mechanisms that such a direct question can set in motion. 'I just wanted to try the water. If I fail, I have nothing to lose' is a common response. It is really a method of taking an each-way bet without losing face. Besides, I did not want a clichéd or short-term unreflective answer such as 'To get my HSC'. I really wanted to get beneath these superficial reasons to the assumptions adult women students hold about education and its rewards for them. Instead I asked about their expectations of returning to study. In this way I was able to discern differences in perceived motivation. Study was either a means to the end of achieving a place in the workforce, improving the present workforce situation, or of gaining personal improvement or fulfilment. Fewer than half of the women in the sample had definite work aspirations, either to re-enter the workforce or to improve their positions within it. Nearly 16 per cent were uncertain whether they wanted a job or not, and over 38 per cent said they definitely did not desire to enter the workforce.

I shall begin my explanation of why women return to study with the reasons which struck me most forcibly.

Housework and family is not enough

Expected outcomes of returning to study, whether for entry into the workforce, improved prospects within it or otherwise, were related, in many cases, to self-image associated with the home. The following comments illustrate my point:

★ I hope there will be the beginning of a change from being Mum to being a person.

★ I want to be recognised as a useful member of the community outside my home environment.

★ I have an inner need to expand my interests and become a person in my own right, rather than just a daughter, wife, or mother.

★ One seems to gain respect in the eyes of family and friends.

All of these comments and many similar ones were written on the questionnaire, often in the margins and in the context of a longer explanation. One woman thanked me for the challenge my questions had offered her in thinking through her own expectations and needs. These hopes for an improved sense of identity are very revealing in what they say about what these women felt about themselves before they returned to study. They provided a valuable clue to be followed up in the interviews which followed concerning the way the woman in the home felt about herself, and the status accorded to her by her family and by society at large. (I use the term 'family' throughout to mean husband, partner, children or extended family.)

Home duties as an occupation is not generally seen as something to be proud of. As much as the type of menial and serving work it entails, the attitudes of some children reinforce its low status. Ann, who in her early fifties was studying for the Higher School Certificate, said, 'I could be the leg of the chair!' I would have laughed with her had it not been for the resentment in her voice.

★ When the children come home, they all say, 'Where is everyone?' I am not a person in their eyes.

During a discussion with women at a women's learning centre, the following comments alerted me to the way many see themselves in relation to other family members:

★ Mother is the gap filler, the time filler-up.

★ If you can't bring in money, you get no respect. I go out to work so I can now ask them to help.

The second comment here suggests that being in the workforce provided a partial solution to the problem of low status within the family, but as this woman was also studying for the HSC, it seems that being at work did not adequately satisfy her need to change her image. In many instances the situation of women in the workplace closely parallels that in the home where service and nurturing are the expected qualifications and activities. These jobs, such as office work, are low on the status scale.

The consciousness of low status ascribed by our present society to the role of housewife is best illustrated by comparing responses to two questions I asked in the questionnaire: What is/ was your occupation? and What is/was the occupation of your mother? Almost one-third of the women in the sample said that their mothers were housewives. Not one of them gave herself that title exclusively. It is possible that mothers acted as role models in the negative sense that their daughters did not want to follow in their footsteps. In fact, Sarah, aged 34, who had returned to study to gain a degree in accounting, expressed this situation precisely:

★ Even when I was quite young, I knew I never wanted to be like my mother, not that she was unhappy, but I knew that sort of life [housewife] was not for me.

Ambivalence about the role of housewife accounts for a high degree of guilt and role conflict experienced by mature-age students. Many mentioned mild to extreme antagonism expressed by family members, including their mothers, to their moving out of their home roles. Add to this ambivalence and conflict the feeling that society does not value work unless it is paid, and we can begin to understand the contribution that returning to study has for the self-image of many women.

In terms of motivation, the following comments made during interviews leave little doubt that many of those who return to study have a very low image of themselves as family members and as individuals:

★ Life was just going past. I was just a housewife. Now I am 'me'. I do want people to look up to me. (Vera, 55)

★ That 'home duties' title is just terrible. I have never put 'HD' but now put 'student'. I don't know whether you have to be a mother to feel that. (Rhonda, 3?)

★ After all those years at home looking after kids, I would think, 'Who am I to say that?' (Rosemary, 41)

★ I think when you're at home with the kids, you think you're not worth much. You don't know much. When you get in a class situation and start getting things right, you think, 'I'm not so silly after all'. (Dora, 43)

★ I'm at home with children *and* I am a student. This creates interest and people want to know about me. (part of a group discussion at a women's learning centre)

★ People around our age didn't have much education. Perhaps they feel mentally inferior. Housewives need some stimulation. They can become depressed. Doing housework, you do lose your identity for a certain number of years. You are a second-class citizen. I'm not interested in the subjects, just the bit of paper so I can say I've got the HSC. (Nell, 48 studying at high-school evening class)

★ I don't feel any longer that I'm just a housewife whose opinions don't count for anything. (a 37-year-old student at a women's learning centre)

People outside the family tend to contribute to the perception of the occupation of housewife as unimportant, as Julie, aged 50, pointed out:

★ When my children went to school, I became involved in community activities. People would say 'What do you do with your time?' The implication was that I was lazy.

Other comments made during a discussion at a learning centre support this attitude to the woman in the home:

★ My husband said jokingly, 'Are you going to be a parasite all your life?'.

★ If you play tennis, you're living a life of leisure. If you have time to play tennis, why aren't you at work?

Educational institutions themselves seem to accept the notion that 'work' is necessarily something done for money outside the home as Pamela, aged 39, observed:

★ My child brought home a questionnaire from the high school which asked, 'Does your mother work?' My reply was that I am not in paid employment but of course I do. I answered 'student' to the question concerning mother's occupation, but realise that is not what they meant. This emphasis on work or home comes up very often in schools. Women are being put upon to do so much—maths help, reading, 'grotty bits and unpaid'. They are expected to do canteen for nothing. Canteen managers get paid but mothers don't.

Lena, aged 44, said succinctly what pervaded many of the interview discussions on motivation when she said that she went through a period of really black depression when she felt that she could have been anybody so long as she filled the role of wife and mother.

That women themselves see their own unpaid work in the home as low in value is evidenced by the comment of Ann, aged 52, who referred to the work she did in the house as 'nothing work', that is, cooking and washing. Vera, aged 55, who was studying to be a library technician, said that she had never worked since she had been married, only as a domestic with a local agency. She had not seen her domestic work, even when paid, as legitimate, presumably because it so resembled what she did in her own home. This situation is exacerbated by changing social expectations. Marie, aged 47, and a student of fine arts, pointed out:

★ People look funny if you say I'm at home, whereas twenty years ago when I first married, they looked askance at you if you had a job.

The role of housewife is certainly a low-status one. Despite studies which reveal her value in economic terms in the capitalist consumer society in which we live, the Royal Commission on Human Relations conducted in 1977 reported that most women in Australia still owe their status and well-being to a father or husband. The same commission noted that mothers, because they lack economic status, are also seen as, and perceive themselves to be, powerless. In her 1979 study, Ann Daniel found that the occupation of housewife had no discernible prestige rating from any section of the Australian community. An overseas study suggested that the status of the non-employed wife may be determined by a combination of the ranking of housewife, conferred status (that is, relevant proximity to people in powerful roles, i.e. male head) and premarriage status which is usually related to the occupation and status of her father. It seems that in the scheme of things, the housewife, so named, has little identity. However, if she combines this task with something more socially acceptable, for example, studying, she can claim the more prestigious title of 'student'.

Education improves status

The relationship between education, self-image and status in society is important. The Royal Commission on Human Relations in 1977 stated that education was one of the principal factors that determines the status of women in our society; it is certainly one of the factors which underlies the prestige of an occupation. Education, occupation, possessions and money are measures of status in our society, so that it is understandable that women will seek education to enhance job prospects. But what of the status of those women who are not in the workforce and who do not aspire to be employed outside the home? If society is seen to ascribe status at least partly by educational level attained, then it is feasible that the adult woman who seeks education, whether she is already in the paid workforce or in the unpaid one in the home, will hold herself in higher esteem because of her achievements. Whether society actually sees her educational attainments as valid contributors to her individual status or whether the occupation of the husband or partner is still a more important measure than her hard-won credential is the subject of interesting debate. Likewise, in the workplace, it is questionable whether a woman's qualifications will in any way challenge the long-established male dominance at the top of the occupational hierarchy. Of course, this may not be a problem for many women, particularly as being in the workforce as a teacher, social worker or librarian is better paid and generally considered more prestigious than being at home.

I feel that while education enhances the view of self, its broader and very important contribution to changes in social attitudes such as those which influence status can only be realised if the woman student learns to question and challenge such underlying social assumptions about status. In other words, she should make the most of education, not only for its potential to improve her self-image and status in the family and wider society, but more importantly by learning the skills of analysis and argument so that she develops the confidence to first challenge, then accept or reject social attitudes.

There is little doubt that the piece of paper, that evidence of years of hard work, is important. Some women were quite certain about the connection between credentials and the way they were seen by others.

★ If you are speaking to an employer, no one's interested if you can speak two languages, but if you say 'I've got the HSC' then in one sentence you've established who you are. It's tangible. (Connie, 48)

Connie saw her personal identity and her status in the workforce as being very closely related to her formal educational credentials. Whether the mature-age student wanted a credential for employment or otherwise, I found a very real sense in which an educational qualification was intrinsically bound up with self-image and perceived status, even within the private social circle of the family. Lena, aged 44, who majored in psychology, first 'tested the water' by sitting in on lectures in the arts faculty without attempting examinations. She felt the need to prove herself to her family and friends and to perform well to get approval. She dared not risk failing an exam. Nell, aged 48, said that the content of the course leading to the credential did not need to be of great interest. She had no real interest in doing legal studies, but found self-satisfaction in achieving a pass in it in the HSC, which she saw as 'an acceptable standard'.

By the time I spoke to Millie, she could reflect on the period of her life when she saw herself only in terms of her academic ability. She had since reconsidered this measurement of self-worth and had rejected one course of further study on the grounds that she now knew how to choose what she really wanted out of education.

★ I was going to be the best housewife and mother but it was just not on. I had a breakdown, then I returned to study. My whole identity was tied up with getting that piece of paper. I was nobody unless I got that piece of paper.

At 36, she had abandoned a Master of Arts degree in favour of a postgraduate women's studies course and had a coordinator's job in a large college. Millie had had long experience as a mature-age student and she admitted that it had taken quite a time for her to realise how dependent she had been on other people's views of her worth. While her education was extremely important in leading her to this understanding, it was no longer as important in itself, as an aid to her self-image.

Many women spoke of the sense of achievement in passing subjects and gaining credentials. This is understandable in view of the fact that children today generally reach a higher level of education than their parents and particularly their mothers. More than half of the women in my sample left school at Year 10 or earlier (see Table 2 in the Appendix). For those who left school at sixteen or earlier, there is the feeling that they could have achieved higher levels at school, if only they had had the chance. Passing subjects and gaining credentials proves that the mind can operate successfully in academic studies. Unlike caring for a family and doing domestic chores, this is measurable. There is a sense in which these women see study with examinations and assessment as providing a purpose, a direction, which is often difficult to see in everyday life at home. Unlike the work of caring for family, it has a tangible goal. It is a way in which women can participate in the competitive society while, at the same time, continuing to practise those skills of sharing of resources and caring for individuals which are the very basis of family life. My insights may seem too deep in the light of the comment that one very honest woman made:

★ I am basically lazy. I need to commit myself to a course with a purpose. I may have given up had there been no exam at the end.

Dependence on the family as a source of interest, sense of self-worth and direction for your life is rather precarious, as one interviewee pointed out. They can be very hurtful without realising it, especially if they laugh at the prospect of mother being able to cope with the demands of the HSC, as one family did. The need to prove that they are capable of doing what they and the wider society see as important and con-tributing to a person's status is a very real motivating force for many women.

A positive improvement in image of self can be seen in the comments of June and Claire, aged 39 and 50 respectively. This is very heartening, but between the lines it is possible to read the message that they had rather low opinions of their positions and little sense of personal identity before they returned to study.

★ The thing that it has done for me is to prove to myself that I am articulate, intelligent and much more perceptive than I ever allowed myself to be. My self-esteem has grown enormously.

★ Self-esteem rises. It's something you want to know yourself. There is a need to achieve, apart from the family. Homemaker is a low status. Study is my own thing.

Many women hoped that study would make them into more interesting people, evidence of both their present view of themselves as not interesting enough, and of the expectation that study would improve that situation.

I've got a job, but . . .

Nearly 44 per cent of women in my sample were working as well as studying, and one-quarter of these women were working full-time. This would seem to question my argument that women return to study because unpaid work in the home earns such low status in our society. It is evident, however, that the secretarial and clerical work they mainly do is seen by them and others to be low in status also, possibly because it is associated with support-ing and serving a person in authority, who is usually a man. Six of those women whose present or previous occupations were in the clerical field desired more advanced clerical work, such as administrative assistant, while twenty of them wished to work in teaching, social work or as librarians; that is, nearly 80 per cent of them aspired to roles in professions where they presumably saw the chance of having a degree of personal authority and thus more status.

I have chosen two statements to illustrate the lack of personal identity that is perceived in clerical and secretarial office work. This factor, combined with the implications of service to a 'boss', is worth pondering.

★ I hate that attitude of being treated like an idiot. You are just a woman to run messages and do the dishes. (Elanor, 32, secretary in a law firm, married)

★ Secretarial work is good to fall back on and I'll do it now if it means I will get some money, but in all the offices I've worked in, men are always the boss and girls are always the secretaries. You could become a managing director's secretary but you could not become a managing director. Primary teaching has always been seen as a career for women. Within the education structure there is opportunity for advancement. There is a female principal at the local school. (Jenny, 27)

Jenny's observations on the limited prospects for individual status as a secretary are supported by a recent study on gender and occupational stratification which found that in the servicing jobs, status is linked to the boss's status and that chances of occupational advances are related to those of the boss. The desire for individual status, rather than status derived from proximity to those in authority, be it the husband or partner at home or the 'boss' at work, can be seen in the desire for work where efforts are measured independently. Preparing for examinations and assessments is work, albeit unpaid, with tangible results which give improved status and improved sense of personal identity to the worker.

Sally, aged 36, who had previously been employed as a kindergarten directress, made a point which provided an insight into the desire for a sense of personal authority and control in the workplace:

★ We are trained to run our own establishment and this gives a sense of control over the situation.

She was studying because she wanted to be a researcher or, if this was not possible, a secondary teacher. She felt the need to pursue education to a higher level than that required for kindergarten teaching. The status of a degree was important to her. Here is evidence of the subtle emphasis on the educational credential as a component in the assessment of the status to which I referred earlier, despite Sally's autonomy in her place of work. It is interesting to note that Sally's husband had a PhD and held a very senior position in the workforce. I shall return to this observation later.

There were 31 women in the sample who were or had been working in secretarial or clerical areas. Most of the occupations to which they aspired, such as administrative assistants, librarians, teachers, counsellors, social workers and psychologists (see Table 1 in the Appendix), can be seen to provide an opportunity for independence of action. The classroom, the library, the consulting room or the office of the administrative or personnel assistant all have a boundary within which the person in charge has autonomy. Thus the large number of office workers seeking qualifications which would lead to alternative work could be motivated by a need for an autonomous identity in the workplace, with esteem and status going to the individual directly rather than through the boss.

It could be argued that a woman has autonomy within the boundaries of her own home, that she has control over her time and contributes equally to decision-making with her husband or partner, but, from the evidence of my research, it seems that this is the ideal rather than the reality. There are many expectations of the woman in the home that have to be recognised in order to understand why so many choose study as a means of gaining some control over their own lives. I discuss these in chapter 3. Perhaps the most obvious one is that she is rarely expected to have activities or interests that compete with the requirements of the family, unless she is paid for them.

Of the six state registered nurses in the research sample, five wanted to work outside the nursing profession. The two state enrolled nurses wanted to move up into the more highly recognised occupation of state registered nurse. The work to which the state registered nurses aspired required academic qualifications, whereas the training they had had as nurses could be seen as a type of apprenticeship. One interviewee referred to the 'manual' aspect of nursing. The alignment of the occupation of nursing with the trades rather than the professions could be an important reason for the desire to move into more academic or administrative fields. The move to take nursing training out of hospitals and into tertiary institutions which is currently under way in New South Wales, Victoria and elsewhere may help to overcome this concept of the profession as non-academic, manual, and by popular assumption lower in status than other caring professions such as social work.

I want a job

★ I think confidence will come with a job. I think it will be linked with being paid for what I do. (Belinda, 40)

Belinda's comment prompted me to consider links between improved self-image and paid work for the women who were studying for the purpose of re-entering the workforce. Her statement illustrates the relationship that exists in our society between view of self and earning money, between the view of self and measurement of the individual's worth which is dictated by our social and economic structure. In the last fifteen years there has been a steady increase in the participation of women in the workforce, but even there, they are generally supporters rather than instigators, assistants rather than administrators. They continue to be involved largely in the areas of education and caring for others which require skills related to dealing with people rather than those involved in administration and decision-making at an executive level. The December 1987 figures from the Commonwealth Department of Employment Women's Bureau indicate that in August 1987, 54.2 per cent of female employees were concentrated in two major occupational groups: clerks and salespersons. While 19 per cent of female employees were in professional and para-professional occupations, 38 per cent of these were teachers and 25.3 per cent were nurses. I do not belittle these types of work, but when society at large does so both by offering lower pay packets and by ascribing lower status to them, it is very difficult for women to assess their own worth without being influenced by the assumptions that underlie this situation.

My own observations of parents' aspirations for their children which I gained during my secondary teaching years prompted me to consider work aspirations in terms of a movement away from work associated with the hands to that more commonly associated with the mind, for example from hairdressing to teaching. It was my experience that parents who worked as tradesmen and manual workers often wanted white-collar jobs for their children. In other words, education was seen as a vehicle of social mobility. Such an outlook can be seen as a response to the generally higher status accorded to professions than to the trades or unskilled occupations, regardless of the bank account of the person working in any of these areas. A recent Australian study illustrates the relationship between knowledge and status even within areas of the teaching professional in the finding that the greater knowledge assumed necessary for secondary teaching in comparison with primary teaching is reflected in its higher status. I am assuming that for most of us, that job for which women take primary responsibility, household administration and housework, is a manual occupation, although considerable cerebral skill can be applied to it to lighten its load—perhaps the most successful one being to ignore all but the most pressing requirements!

Table 1 in the Appendix uses either present or most recent occupation of the women in the sample as the basis for comparison with what jobs they aspire to as a result of their studies. It illustrates the general desire for upward mobility, and in some cases the desire to move away from manual work can be noticed. Another possibility arises out of the comparison between past and future occupations, and that is the desire to gain more recognition for, and perhaps personal satisfaction from, one's work. As I have suggested, this is most probably associated with the desire for not only more status but more autonomy in the workplace. Most of the occupations aspired to require initiative and organisational skills which are practised in the home but rarely recognised for their worth.

Only two of the 46 women I interviewed broached the subject of job-sharing with their partners. Their return to study to gain qualifications was directly related to a view of their family life where the partners shared all aspects from childcare to provision of income. Millie, aged 36, whose husband had chosen to be employed part-time in the paid workforce and part-time in the home, said:

★ The status of being breadwinner means an awful lot to me. I could not be unemployed again.

Sarah, aged 34 and studying to be an accountant, had similar goals:

★ I feel I would have really made it then if I could work and support the family and my husband could be home or in part-time work.

These attitudes suggest to me that these two women sought to establish their individual status in the workplace on grounds similar to those upon which the male status is assessed, that is, occupation and education. Role reversal is one means of attaining a satisfactory sense of self-worth, but it is also important to consider whether one must use a place in the paid workforce as a measurement of worth. Presumably, the husbands of Millie and Sarah based their sense of identity on other criteria. For Rita, a divorcee of 32 with two children, studying to gain a good job was directly related to the way in which she wished to be seen by her son and the wider society, that is, as a paid worker:

★ The status of paid employment is quite different from 'on a pension'. I don't want my son to have to say that his mother is on a pension.

The important requirement in thinking about self-image and status is to *understand* who and what dictates these measurements of a person's value, and then to freely *choose* what path to follow. In the workplace, in social situations and in the home there is a 'pecking order'. Women and men see themselves in relation to it, accept it, reject it or try to transcend it by whatever means they consider effective. The social hierarchy is based on such criteria as wealth, prestige, occupation, education and proximity to power. When a person, male or female, has a low-status occupation, such as unskilled labourer or domestic servant, it can be assumed that he or she will be near the bottom of the ladder. I have already discussed the status of the housewife in Australian society and her reliance on her husband or partner for her status. Even the possibility of occupation-based status for women is problematic in that, besides the tendency for females in similar jobs to males to be accorded slightly lower status, many women with families occupy part-time jobs which rarely carry very much prestige. Furthermore, women tend to choose jobs that will fit in with their family commitments, suggesting that the choice of occupation may not reflect their potential in the employment market if they were to compete without such commitments. Is it any wonder that there is a dilemma in assessing the status of women? Is it any wonder that the women themselves feel the need to improve their positions in the social hierarchy? But what are the options?

Option A: marriage. A woman can marry into a high-status family. It has been claimed, in fact, that education for girls is seen by many families to be a means by which such an outcome will occur, in other words, that education prepares them for the marriage rather than the labour market. In my research, I included only women over 25, the majority of whom were married, and some to men in high-status occupations, such as doctors. But my findings suggest that status thus achieved does not necessarily ensure a positive self-image. In fact, 'marrying up' often brings an added sense of personal incompetence for a number of reasons generally related to family background and standards of education (see Table 2 in the Appendix).

History has repeated itself in that daughters, like their mothers, have lower educational standards than their husbands, although the younger generation of women far exceed their mothers in years of schooling. Husbands also have higher educational attainments than fathers. This factor can be accounted for historically with gradual increase in participation in secondary education by both sexes since the proliferation of government high schools in Australia in the early 1960s. More girls than boys now take Year 12 examinations in some states in Australia. This fact could be interpreted as an indication that for girls and women, education is a very important element in the subjective assessment of self. This historical explanation may be sufficient to clarify the differences between the generations, but the fact still remains that wives in the research sample had achieved much lower levels of education than their husbands. Of husbands of participants in my study, 42.5 had been tertiary-trained, but 85.2 per cent of wives had not. In society where status is related, among other things, to occupation and education, this discrepancy cannot be easily overlooked. In addition, other factors, such as government legislation for equal opportunity for women, the entry of increasing numbers of women into state and federal politics, dissatisfaction with low-status jobs available to women and the general pervasiveness of the ideas of the women's movement into many areas, for example, childcare, in which women are vitally interested, all contribute to a greater awareness of the differences in recognition and opportunity which society affords men and women. Inconsistencies in status, particularly if the woman's sense of worth is not adequately bolstered by recognition of her competence by her husband and family, can lead to a desire to change the situation. Education is seen to be the key, either by proving her ability to her family, or by providing the means to enter the workforce, or both.

Option B: entering the workforce. I have already mentioned some of the drawbacks associated with being a part-time, female, married-with-children member of the workforce. There are also a number of problems for those women without children who are in full-time jobs, not the least of which is the expectation that they will not pursue a career with the same single-mindedness as a man because they might decide to have children. Entering the workforce, however, or trying to upgrade one's position within it, is another option to try to improve one's status. This improvement may be mainly economic, but having money of one's own *does* help to relieve that sense of dependence which often undermines one's feeling of self-worth.

I have noted the types of jobs that women in the sample had in mind (see Table 1 in the Appendix), but notice how few of the 70 women aspired to professions other than the traditional ones of teaching, social work, counselling. A woman may improve her status, but generally only within the confines dicatated by the social and economic structure in which we live. This may satisfy her, but again, she may not have considered her aspirations in this light. If she is looking for more status within the family, the workplace and in the wider community, she may have to reassess the criteria upon which she will gain such status. If her work is an extension of her caring and nurturing home role, and if she carefully arranges it so that it does not intrude into the routine of the home and family, will the family think of her any differently? Likewise, if her family commitments restrict her involvement in her work, for example, being unable to attend late meetings or weekend seminars, will she ever attain a high-status job?

There are many reasons why women tend to lean towards the caring and serving jobs. Teaching fits in with their own children's timetables. Women are interested in people and issues rather than economics and structures. Previous education limits retraining in anything that requires maths. Women are not technically minded. But who established these reasons and are they relevant to every woman? Certainly the caring, organisational and administrative skills she practises in the community and very often in the workplace are worthy ones and very important in our society, but there must be a place for these as well as newly learned skills, such as computer programming, in the workplace. In other words, it is not enough for a woman glibly to assume that 'I am no good at maths'. Most likely she suffered the same educational experiences as most other mature-age women in that she was not encouraged to study maths and sciences unless she was exceptional or her parents insisted on it. There are bridging and preparatory maths/science classes available at a number of centres in Melbourne where there is no pressure to pass exams. They try to overcome that assumption that these subjects belong in the realms of men and younger women who might have studied them at school. The world of business and industry would benefit if it could use the abilities of women to plan time use, organise other people and keep a sense of cohesion in a group. They have generally had years of experience observing their mothers and practising these skills themselves. All that is required is the understanding that these doors to non-traditional careers are not closed except by our own ideas about our abilities.

Option C: education. Education is another method by which a woman can try to improve her status. She can educate herself and gain a credential which society may recognise as a measure of worth. For a number of women whom I interviewed, this was the means to gain respect from males.

★ One way you can get respect from males is if you have similar qualifications; you can speak and they will accept you as nearly equal. You can use the same language.

★ People (especially male) look at me differently and with more respect now that they think I have a brain—not an aspect that I necessarily enjoy.

These may be options which women have for improving their status in the social hierarchy, but the *reasons why* many women have a sense of low self worth still needs further investigation. For over half of the respondents, a desire to return to work or to gain a higher position in the workforce had not been a definite motivating factor. When asked what outcome was expected if not a place in the workforce, almost one-third offered explanations relating to self-fulfilment and personal satisfaction. I want to consider here what this means in terms of how these women feel about themselves before seeking this result from returning to study.

The late Abraham Maslow classified and described five human needs which he claimed influenced behaviour. There are five levels in what he called the 'hierarchy of needs'. At the bottom of the pyramid are physiological needs, for example, food and shelter. If you cannot satisfy these basic needs, it is unlikely that you will be storing up anything for the future, that is, satisfying the next need, that of security. People motivated by security needs will often remain in monotonous, unsatisfying jobs for years to ensure that they do not become destitute. There is little time to consider other needs in this situation. The woman, for example, who works all day in a factory or office at the same time as caring for her family because they need the money for basic essentials such as food, shelter and education can think only of the practicalities of fitting all her responsibilities for one day into the allotted 24 hours. If she does reflect on her position, she rarely has the opportunity or the energy to do anything about it. The family is both the central commitment and by necessity the group which must satisfy her social needs, the next in Maslow's hierarchy of needs.

While Maslow presented his ideas on needs and motivation in terms of stages, it would be simplistic to imagine that there is a clear point at which one says, 'Now, on to the task of satisfying my next need'. There is a degree of overlapping and, in some cases, the basic needs for food, shelter and security recur and thus absorb energy that previously had been spent on satisfying the 'higher' needs, that is social, ego and self-fulfilment needs.

Social needs follow the satisfaction of the 'lower' needs and manifest themselves in the desire for acceptance by others. Belonging to a group entails accepting written or unwritten rules of conduct which most people accept because of their felt need to belong to such a group. The family is a good example. Roles and expectations are preset, generally by historical or cultural precedents. Desire to remain within a traditionally acceptable group is very strong, but in some cases the next need discussed by Maslow, the ego need, is not satisfied within the group. I have found that, for some women, the family is the group in which social acceptance is primarily sought. They use a criterion accepted by society, education, as a means of adding value to their image in their own eyes and, they hope, in the eyes of the family. This measurement of worth, education, and particularly credentials is also used by women whose need for acceptance and thus status extends to the wider sphere of the paid workplace. The family, the workplace, community life, are all places where men and women meet, but everywhere the status of the man is perceived to be higher than that of the woman. Consider terms such as 'the breadwinner', 'the boss', 'the director'. Do we think of them as women or as men? Many women see education and credentials as a way of closing this status gap.

The ego need has two facets: self-esteem and status. We all need affirmation, that is, recognition by others that we are worthwhile. This gives us a sense of self-esteem. What we *are* in society's terms usually relates to our role, rather than to our personalities, and therein lies a very real problem for some women. According to Maslow, 'the desire for . . . prestige . . . status . . . dominance, recognition, attention, importance . . . or appreciation' are important contributors to our self-esteem which we must achieve for ourselves. Mere flattery is not enough, nor is a patronising recognition of our abilities. A place in the workforce might be seen to improve our image. It certainly improves the income and often helps to alleviate a feeling of dependence. A great number of married women are presently in the workforce. The figures for November 1985 show that women comprise 78.8 per cent of the part-time workforce, with married women accounting for 57.4 per cent of all part-time employees. Nearly 44 per cent of the women in my research sample were in the workforce and were studying at the same time, which suggests to me that being employed outside the home does not necessarily satisfy the ego needs. For many women, these ego needs are not satisfied within the home, the workplace or social circles because of the relatively lower status accorded them in all three areas. Social attitudes towards the status of work done by women are evidenced by lower pay than the male in the workforce and by the very low status ascribed to the position of the woman at home.

A study of social stratification in Australia suggests that 'the concept most central to status is prestige, and by definition, social prestige rests on qualitative attitudes such as esteem, deference, admiration, exclusiveness, appreciation, honour, respect, condescension and dignity'. It follows that if these attitudes are not present, or only marginally so, in one's perception of how one is seen by others, the self-image as well as status is low. Whether the mature-age student embarks on a course of study as a means to gaining a position in the paid workforce, or improving one she already has, or whether the occupation 'student' earns enough respect in itself, I have little doubt that one of the basic motivators is a desire to improve self-image, and, in the wider context, status in society. In other words, I have found that for many women, ego needs are not satisfied in the home, the social circle or the workplace.

The highest need in Maslow's hierarchy is the desire for self-fulfilment. This is seen as the ultimate need to be satisfied in order to reach one's full potential. Pursuing it takes the form of trying to perfect the existing job, learning new skills, or becoming a better or more interesting person. Nearly one-third of the respondents to the questionnaire stated 'self-fulfilment' 'gaining more confidence' or 'becoming a more interesting person' as their expectation of returning to study. But by whose standards would they be fulfilled, or become more interesting? On what criteria would their newfound confidence rest? I shall return to these questions later in this chapter.

In our society, education and occupation are the most important factors in assessing status. Education is open to all who have satisfied their basic security needs, male or female. For this reason I suggest that there are two possible alternative sequences by which women are motivated to fulfil their higher needs. First, they attempt to develop their full intellectual potential as a means of gaining recognition in a society that values years of education and credentials as well as occupation as a measure of status. An improved self-image is then a product of this achieved status. Second, the social needs for acceptance by others, for belonging and for giving and receiving friendship and affection are not met, or are insufficiently met, in the family and immediate social circle, so that the confidence in oneself that would develop under such conditions is often lacking. For some this acceptance by others is seen in terms of recognition of worth through credentials, while for others the educational environment itself provides the necessary support and encouragement to improve the sense of self-worth.

The comments referred to earlier, for example, 'My whole life was tied up with getting that piece of paper', which emphasised the relationship between gaining credentials and a sense of personal identity, confirm my proposition. For some women, the supportive environment in which they learn develops a self-confidence which is only indirectly related to study or the gaining of credentials. By becoming aware of the assumptions which underlie their desire for education, for example, that it will in itself enhance their status, and by sharing and analysing their experiences as paid and unpaid workers, many women come to value themselves more *before* they embark on formal education. Some deliberately choose not to follow that road but to use their newly recognised skills in other areas. Affirmation from others can come from a group who share learning and life experiences; it can come by means of a credential which reflects society's criteria of worth; or it can come by a combination of these two means. Whether you see formal education alone as a means of self-fulfilment depends very much on which perspective you take.

In the learning group it is important that the facilitator understands her own perspectives, that is, that she has carefully analysed her assumptions about the role. She must ensure that the adults she is working with learn to value their own experiences and develop confidence in forming and expressing opinions in an unthreatening atmosphere. When people who lack confidence join a group, there is a danger that they will transfer their dependence to that group. This is a retrograde step and one which can be avoided if the learning experience fosters careful analysis and criticism of all assumptions based on an understanding of the types of influences that contribute to their formation.

No woman is an island

★ My children say I'm going for my Monday night 'fix' when I go to classes. At first I chose those women near my own age because they knew what it was like to feel like a fool. Last year I found I could talk to the younger ones too. I have a strong sense of belonging with other mature-age women students. (Joan, 52)

The social needs for acceptance by others, which Maslow argues precedes ego and self-fulfilment needs, for many women are not always satisfactorily met in participating in their children's school activities, family associations, or women's social groups. For Sally, aged 36, going to classes is the highlight of her social week because she says she can talk on an interesting level, rather than 'how many dirty nappies I washed this week'.

Deirdre, in her late forties, raised an interesting point when she said to me that she had two roles: those on her own level and the 'other'. She went on to explain that she felt she could really be herself with women who could discuss matters of broad interest, but at the same time she was quick to point out that she did not mean to belittle her other role. She simply 'switched off' from one role and 'turned on' to the other when required.

I sense that much of the social contact women crave in returning to study has to do with the fact that they have outgrown, or have never happily fitted into, the role that has been prescribed for them in the home, or the one they have in the paid workforce. In a long letter about her experiences as a mature-age student, one woman told me.

★ I've enjoyed making new friends of all ages. And it's the one place I can walk into and be 'me', not mother, wife, daughter, etc. It's also the one place I can go and completely forget my problems (almost).

Another woman said that she enjoyed the company of other women of a wide range of backgrounds and interests not always available in the local community or among personal friends. There was a sense of belonging expressed in many comments in this vein—belonging in a way that has to do with being part of a world outside the home and nurturing a previously hidden or undiscovered personal identity. It was often in discussions about the need for friendships based on shared learning experiences outside the home that I gained a picture of the social pressures and expectations that weigh heavily on some women. It became clear to me that many mature-age women become students in search of social contact and personal identity because of a sometimes unrecognised oppression at home. (The attitudes and expectations of husbands, children and extended family towards the wife and mother who returns to study are considered in chapter 3.) During a discussion with a group at a women's learning centre (see p. 56), there were some very revealing comments about the connection between a feeling of low status and the need to make contact with a group which will accept the individual without reference to her domestic role.

★ You can try ideas here that you would not think of saying outside. You're not someone's wife and mother.

Given the generally low perception of self within the family

which many of the respondents expressed, together with the
lower educational and status levels occupied by them in
comparison with their husbands and often with their children, it
is likely that those who would see social contact as the reason for
seeking education are actually looking for the environment in
which they can begin to value theselves more. There is evidence
of a need for acceptance as a thinking, autonomous person,
rather than as the stereotype of the nurturing, selfless 'Angel in
the House' to which Virginia Woolf referred in 1931:

★She was intensely sympathetic. She was immensely charming. She
was utterly unselfish. She excelled in the difficult art of family life. She
sacrificed herself daily. If there was a chicken, she took the leg; if there
was a draught she sat in it—in short she was so constituted that she
never had a mind or a wish of her own, but preferred to sympathize
always with the mind or wishes of others.

Although Virginia Woolf was describing the housewife of the
late Victorian household, vestiges of this image remain with
many women.

I can see two possibilities for new friendships when women
return to study because they need more social contact. It has to
do with the nature of the task they set themselves. If their first
action is to commit themselves to preparation for a credential,
they are very quickly involved in a time-consuming, competitive,
absorbing and often lonely exercise. Friendships do develop,
based on shared problems of shortage of time, assessments, and
so on, but these women rarely have the time or the opportunity
to get to know the backgrounds or life experiences of their new
friends. This need not be so. If the learning environment is one
in which their life experiences are drawn upon in relation to
issues or problems raised in the subject matter, the people in the
group become involved in each other's ideas and opinions. The
teacher in such a group must be skilled in fostering critical
analysis and discussion and guiding the participants back to the
issue from time to time to point out the relevance of their
personal experiences. Friendships formed in this way are based
on understanding of a person's values and opinions, on shared
experiences and mutual encouragement encountered in a new

way of life; they can also be based on a deeper understanding of the backgrounds, life experiences, assumptions and values of the people gained as friends. The latter basis for friendship would seem more likely to have a lasting positive effect on the sense of personal identity and worth because it would encompass facets of life outside those evident in the usually hurried contacts made when attending lectures and classes.

An approach to adult learning which allows for the use of valuable life experiences in understanding subject matter is encapsulated in a statement by the Association of Neighbourhood Learning Centres:

★ Courses are *only the means* by which people come together to share their problems, to verbalise their needs and to gain confidence in themselves as socially necessary human beings, to stimulate awareness of their rights as individuals and to develop a social consciousness as people and members of a wider community. [their emphasis]

The joy of learning

A small number of women expressed their delight in the 'sheer joy of learning'. Some were women who saw study filling a gap in their lives after retirement from paid work, or in their later years when their children had left home. Finding out about the world around them, about historical movements, about ideas and philosophies, all were seen as satisfying an innate desire to know more. For example, Wanda, aged 40, felt that her outlook had been very much enriched:

★ Things that would have been very obscure before I feel I can really grasp now.

The pursuit of knowledge for its own sake suggests a liberal view of education perhaps more appropriately linked with distant times, such as fifth-century Athens or Renaissance Rome. Education for pleasure was for the well-to-do and there were slaves to perform menial and serving work. Today many women have to juggle their domestic chores and paid work with essay writing and reading. At government level, suggested changes in tertiary education by the Department of Employment, Education and Industry so that it is more related to the needs of industry would seem to devalue education for its own sake. With the possibility of the reintroduction of university fees, not to mention the administration fee which is already payable, I fear for the woman who simply enjoys learning.

Social attitudes often tend to dampen the joy of learning. Achievement must be measured. The sister of one of the interviewees very deliberately pointed out to her that:

★ You could go on doing classes and courses, but who are you if you haven't go that piece of paper?

Most women in my sample put themselves through the gruelling tests of examination and essay-writing. Only two who said they had returned to study for the joy of learning did not attempt exams. A number of respondents to the questionnaire had had previous adult education in non-accredited classes, such as book groups, but the interviews revealed a need, in many cases, for the added discipline of preparation for examinations. I do not deny the joy of learning, but I do suggest that it is often combined with joy of achieving. True scholarship requires a degree of analysis and reflection which is difficult to obtain when one is hell-bent on achieving a credential in spite of difficulties such as conflict of roles, guilt and shortage of time, among other things. If the student has unlimited time to pursue her studies, it is then possible to overcome the feeling of skimming over or treating subject material superficially, a problem that quite a few women mentioned.

There is also a certain joy in feeling free to use one's time in a way which is satisfying to oneself. Study is a legitimate activity which can justify changes in priorities of time use. One woman, for example, said that she no longer felt guilty reading a book during the day now she was studying HSC. Another claimed that she felt she could do what she most liked doing (print-making) without feeling she was wasting time because she was doing it as part of a fine arts degree. Obviously these women had internalised a notion of valid use of their time which excluded pursuing intellectual interests which gave them joy. This means that a sense of autonomy, of control over one's own time, is weakened by other social forces that dictate how women should spend their time. The self-image, then, is relatively low if study has to be used to validate one's use of time.

Further, for the woman who needs society's recognition of her abilities, it is unlikely that she would be satisfied with intrinsic reward, although this is an important factor, unless of course she already valued herself highly. I have found little evidence of such high self-image in the interviews, even when speaking with women whose husbands occupy high positions on the social scale.

The reward of returning to study is not simply 'intrinsic'. These women are gathering knowledge and understanding of the world on which they can form their own opinions, and thus improve their sense of self-worth. The joy of learning, per se, is associated with the learning that takes place, of course, but it is the effect on self that is most important. Indeed, there is evidence that when the learning environment *does not* actively stimulate discussion and reflection, all the knowledge in the world does not increase general confidence in self. Joy, without improved self-image, is surely diminished.

Rhonda's story gives weight to my claim. She was 32 years old when I interviewed her, had been married for eleven years and had no children. She had been a secretary for eleven years and her last position three years before had been as a liaison officer. She did four subjects for the HSC over two years at a high-school evening class before beginning an arts degree while working, first full-time and then part-time. The final two years of the BA degree were completed full-time as she resigned from her position in the workforce and her present study was directed towards a Bachelor of Letters degree. She was ambivalent about a career; in fact, she said that she was not ambitious and loved studying. Her expressed motivation for returning to study was 'to keep the rust out of my brain', and a similar fear 'of becoming a cabbage' had kept her going, although she was extremely shy. When she began her study for a Bachelor of Letters, she told herself, 'you've got a BA; you're going to be different now, not shy'. But it didn't happen. She did claim that having a BA had given her more confidence in some situations, but not in the academic one. Despite this, she had satisfied her own image of herself as someone with an active brain. Is this intrinsic reward? Perhaps she felt joy in achieving despite her shyness. It harks back to that fear that 'I am not good enough unless I have proved it by gaining that degree'. I think the environment in which adults learn should foster confidence in self through understanding the forces that help to determine how we see the world and our place in it. Making considered choices as a result of this brings real joy.

I've reached a stage

Anyone who has read *Passages* by Gail Sheehy will have tried to place herself into one of the stages she describes. She will also have had some reaction to her placing 'mid-life' at the age of 35, although this is halfway to those threescore years and ten. Having chosen the 'care-giver' role by the age of 30, most women in her study sought a new direction on reaching forty. Nearly two-thirds of them had gone back to school or sought jobs, seven at 30, fourteen at 35 and 35 at forty. She claims that the question 'Why am I doing this?' and 'What do I really believe in?' are asked by everyone. I am not sure that such deeply searching questions are always asked, or if they are, are answered with any critical understanding of the social forces which shape our belief systems and our vision of self. Instead, the criterion upon which society at large places such importance in assessing status, that is, education, is *automatically* sought by many of those who vaguely or strongly feel a sense of inadequacy or powerlessness. For this reason, the gaining of credentials assumes an importance which can often deflect the adult woman student from confronting the situations in her own life which underlie her uncertainty.

With this assumption in mind, I did investigate whether

returning to study could be seen as a 'stage of life' phenomenon, that is, whether arriving at a certain stage actually contributed to the decision to act. As caring for children is such an important consideration for most women, I looked at the ages of children of the women in the sample to try to determine whether that had some bearing on a perceived 'stage of life' for women, and thus on their desire to seek a new direction through education (see Table 3 in the Appendix).

The number of women with children of twelve years or under (more than half of those women in the sample who had children) supports the notion that they were preparing for the next stage of their lives when the children would be less dependent. There is, however, another possibility: that they were acting on a feeling of inadequacy when their child-rearing phase was at its peak. Two interviewees supported this interpretation with the following comments:

★ I felt I had a very satisfying life as wife and mother but after fifteen years of marriage I became depressed. I went to a psychiatrist who suggested that I needed to grow and develop. He pushed me. (Lena, 44. Her children were 11 and 13 when she returned to study.)

★ One doctor gave me anti-depressant pills when I went to him feeling very depressed. Another told me it was up to me to decide what I wanted to do with my life, to think about my future. (Belinda, 40. Her children were 8 and 6 when she returned to study.)

Studies on suburban neurosis and depression in women support the notion that a sense of isolation from the rest of society leads to some sort of action. As Dianne, aged 42 and divorced, suggested, many women turn to drugs or drink. She returned to study. During a discussion at a learning centre, one woman student saw that she had arrived at a very definite stage in her life:

★ You've had your children. You've been married for some time and you become aware of the cracks in the facade of your husband. You ask yourself, 'Will I have an affair or will I return to study?'

There was only one woman I interviewed who said that she had positively chosen a career rather than having children. This decision was not made without her enduring considerable pressure from her parents and friends. At 36, Liz was taking a degree in business administration which would be the means to promotion in her semi-government managerial job. Most women, however, have their families first, then return to study. Lorna, who at 37 was divorced with three children, worked as a secretary. At the same time, she undertook study for an arts degree part-time. She said she felt compelled to have a family first, but she continued to read books on English and history during that time, knowing that at some stage she would continue her education.

As I suggested, some women do consider the next stage of their lives while their children are at their most dependent. There is a sense in which these women are pre-empting the 'empty nest' and sensing a coming loss of identity which they presently relate to being a mother. A comment on a questionnaire suggested that study provides a valuable transition from home duties and mothers' clubs to broader aspects of life by providing company, knowledge of the world and possibly a place in the paid workforce. Beatrice, 35 and divorced, asked herself, 'What am I going to do when the children get older?' Another divorcee, Ann, aged 42, had a similar sense of 'the next stage' when she said:

★ There's a turning point when your children get older when, if you don't do something for yourself, you stagnate.

'When the children leave, I want something to go on to' was the comment of Julie, married and aged fifty.

Preparation for when the family have grown up as well as a generally low sense of identity during the child-rearing stage means that many women add study to their already busy lives in preparation for the future. This observation, and indeed my own experience, led me to question time use and priorities during this care-giving period of women's lives. The conflict between care-giving and satisfying one's own desires is epitomised in the comment of Sarah, aged 34:

★ Study is a sort of halfway house; you can satisfy everybody. It's not threatening—you're not earning money and maybe you won't make it.

Sarah's last sentence indicated to me that she herself was prepared to let her success or otherwise be determined by an outside mediator, in this case a system of assessment devised by educational institutions. I did not press her further, but, in the light of her excellent academic results, I assumed that her own sense of self-worth was being adequately enhanced. But it was evident that she sensed a hope in others close to her that the whole nasty business might go away.

For those who had stayed married, or in long-term relationships, the rate of their personal development was generally tied to the requirements, needs or demands of their partners and children. These could be explicit or implicit, but in either case inhibiting to any sense of autonomous control of their own life options. The most insidious aspect of this tie is the assumption, often accepted by the adult student herself, that the time she spends on her own development is not legitimately spent, that is, that it has a little real purpose or outcome. A conversation with adult women students at a women's learning centre revealed their experiences of the perceived non-importance of women's time in the eyes of their partners. The consensus was that most husbands see study as 'a little bit of a hobby'. The husband of 60-year-old arts student Janet, who had retired from his work, decried her waste of time because 'she was only doing it because she liked it'. Presumably it would have been more virtuous had she done something she did not like. Under such conditions, the need to improve status within the family and the wider society, and to make their actions more legitimate by obtaining credentials, can be better understood.

It would seem, though, that many mature-age students do little *within* the home to claim the time used in studying as legitimate. For example, one 50-year-old respondent said:

★ I bent over backwards to show that it [study] was not going to make any difference to anyone else. I wrote during the night and early morning. I made no difference to my life.

The 'no difference to my life' here probably means 'no difference to the lives of other family members'. In many of the responses there was evidence of self-deprivation discussed in a way that indicated that it was a normal, even necessary, state. Heather said, 'There is no change in my life. I simply get up earlier'. But it was with some bitterness that Joan stated, 'It is the things I do for myself that suffer'. Developing the ability to make use of short spaces of time, or dovetailing household tasks and study, was another method devised to keep the amount of apparent change in the home to a minimum.

Another important priority is money. The financial aspect of spending for fees and books often uncovered another area of dependence and conflict of priorities. A nurse retraining in community health had this to say:

★ It is difficult for women to spend money on themselves. It is all right for husbands or children, but for a purely selfish thing like personal growth, even fees for studying and books, even if there is plenty of money in the house, it seems to be a real thing that they don't think they're worth it.

Consider what the imposition of tuition or administration fees would do to maintain and reinforce this feeling!

As I have suggested, the 'empty nest' stage is sometimes planned for while the children are dependent. For others, like Caroline, aged 43, it was a conscious decision to wait 'until the children were under control'. Two interviewees in their fifties, Claire and Carol, felt there was a gap in their lives after their children left home and asked the question, 'What is there for me?' The children of nearly a quarter of the women in the sample were aged seventeen or over, which does suggest that 'the empty nest' may be a contributing factor to the decision to return to study.

His wife or myself

Thirty women in the sample were separated or divorced, and 23 of them had been in that state for five years or less. Almost half of them had been separated or divorced for two years or less. The comments of some of these twelve separated or divorced students who volunteered to be interviewed throw some light on whether this life crisis acted as a motivating force for them to return to study. The converse, that returning to study contributed to marriage breakdown, is discussed later.

It is difficult to single out one factor which becomes the catalyst for separation or divorce, but when attitudes were discussed, it was sometimes possible to see a desire for personal growth being stifled by attitudes of husbands. For example, Beatrice, a divorcee of four years, aged 35, said that she had suggested two or three years before her marriage broke up that she wanted to return to study for the HSC. Her husband's reply was angry:

★ Why should I pay for you to be educated? Your family should have done that. Why aren't you happy doing the housework?

In insecure and deteriorating marital situations, Elizabeth, 34, Connie, 48, and Penelope, 51, felt the need for social and economic independence and sought study as therapeutic and expedient. On the other hand, Lorna, 37, enrolled for the HSC soon after her marriage but dropped out at that stage because of her husband's derogatory remarks. She returned to complete it and go on to an arts degree after her divorce.

More common was the sequence of separation or divorce followed by a return to study. Eight women spoke of this situation, some referring to their need to study as a 'survival' move either in the sense of finding social contact and support or as a necessary means to getting back into the workforce. While one woman spoke of her severe depression and inertia after her husband moved out, others felt a new freedom to lead their own lives. Two women spoke of not being allowed to study when their husbands were there. The acknowledgment by Dianne, 42, 'I was either his wife or myself. I had a choice' aptly illustrates the types of implicit pressures exerted on many women who try to develop according to their individual needs.

There appears to be no definable stage of life when women return to study. Rather, an awakening or recognition of the need for a sense of personal identity is generally the catalyst. As Moira, aged 37, perceptively noted:

★ You have to be at a stage of your life where you are prepared to open your mind to other things. It has to be gradual as you are defensive of where you are.

I'm getting older

Although there was a sharp fall away in numbers of women over 50 in the sample (see Table 4 in the Appendix), there is little to suggest that reaching a specific age is in itself a significant factor in deciding to return to study. The combined 36-44-year grouping had by far the largest percentage, offering some support for the notion of preparation for the time when the family leave home. There is also, as I mentioned before, the possibility that this period when the family is dependent is also the time when the mother's sense of autonomy or personal identity is at a low ebb. As one woman said, 'I am getting older and who wants a 45-year-old highly trained psychologist with no practical experience?' Excerpts from interviews already quoted suggest that there is a need to establish criteria for self-worth other than those pertaining to husband and family. As Lena commented, 'My home is important, but I am not just a housewife'.

Other reasons

A study of mature-age women returning to study in the United States found that a disorienting experience often leads to self-examination and a different direction in life. Five events can be seen as disorienting experiences: marital breakdown has been considered already. Widowhood brought similar needs for emotional independence for two women in the study. Advice from doctors and social workers about illness and depression has been seen to contribute to a decision to return to study, and, in fact, two interviewees stated that it was the imposed rest associated with illness that gave them time to reflect on their lives. Retirement from work also gave time for reflection. 'What have I done with my life?' was the question asked by Lorna, a retired bookkeeper, aged sixty.

Only one interviewee spoke of the experience of not being able to have children as a motivating force. She said she wanted to take her mind off her problem and did not want to become obsessed with it.

Direct challenges from others which lead to self-examination take a number of forms. A domestic in a hospital was told by the sister-in-charge that she was wasting her talents in such menial work; a lecture by a woman at a local community centre prompted self-examination for another; contact with university students who worked at the same factory awakened one adult student to another world; for yet another, reading *Dibs in Search of Self* led to a re-evaluation of life's paths. A trauma experienced by an expectant single mother regarding the sincerity of her child's father eventually worked to her advantage. She was philosophical and a little grateful in her recognition that 'perhaps that was the beginning'.

No doubt each one of us could think of deeply buried doubts and unmet needs which have prompted some of our actions. That motives for returning to study are complex, and that they change, or are reassessed, during the course of study, has been observed in my research. One respondent commented in reply to an open-ended question on experiences as a mature-age student:

★ I think many excuses are used to justify one's return to study, not only to family members, but to oneself. By doing this, I feel one can find oneself doing a course or subject that one doesn't want to do. In answering Question 33 [relating to expected job opportunities], my present study will lead to job opportunities, but it is not my main reason for doing it.

She did not pinpoint an initial reason for returning to study, but I found her language interesting—'justify', for example, suggests that one is defending a position. Another woman confirmed that the experience of study altered her reasons for continuing with it. She said:

★ When I began to study in 1976 it was to prove to myself that I could do it, that is, I had a hang-up about being uneducated. This reason changed with time and the reason now is to gain an interesting and challenging position in the workforce.

Each one of us has a number of personal reasons why we have

returned to study or are considering it, reasons which are tied to our personalities and the way we see ourselves. It is important to consider these reasons carefully, and to think about our expectations of education as an adult. Ideally, the learning environment to which we return should help to clarify our understanding of our motives and aspirations first, so that we can confidently choose to continue along the rigorous path of higher education, undertake technical or business training, take up subjects which interest us (not necessarily for assessment), or use the skills we already possess with more confidence.

PART II
WHAT TO EXPECT
WHEN YOU DO

TWO
MEETING WOMEN'S NEEDS

'In childminding you see people and know they are just like you. They often come because of the creche and finish up doing secondary-level courses.'

The semantic debate on the distinction between education and learning could constitute a whole chapter in itself, and, in various forms, is well documented in adult and continuing education literature. Education can encourage learning of the kind that leads to ongoing critical thinking about the student's circumstances, even the educational environment in which she is participating. On the other hand, it can encourage an acceptance of its own worth to the point where it becomes simply a means to an end, a credential and thus a recognised place in our hierarchical society. I certainly do not belittle the seeking of qualifications but when, as I have found, that act of returning to study is so closely related to improving the image of self, I feel it is vital for not only women but all adults who approach formal education in this way to consider the broader implications of their desire for credentials. This is particularly important when a place in the workforce is definitely not the expected outcome of study. An understanding of how our society works, the places of education, marriage and the workplace in it, and of one's own contribution to it is an important prerequisite for undertaking a course of study. I spoke in the Introduction of some folly of mine. It has to do with not understanding the distinction between education and learning. In my thesis, I examined this question at some length in terms of perception of student needs, both by the student herself and the provider of adult education. In this chapter I wish to throw some light on the different venues, ranges of subjects and teaching methods which are available for women who return to study in the hope that this will help the would-be student to understand and recognise her needs, particularly in the light of this distinction between education and learning.

Educational practice reflects educational philosophy, whether stated or not. Curricula offered, methods of teaching and the physical environment in which classes take place all reveal in some way the ideological and philosophical perspective from which the provider views the needs of adult students. One thing is certain: *access* to education in itself does not overcome assumptions about what women want to learn, nor does it overcome the internalised view of self that the adult student carries with her as a result of her experiences as a daughter, wife, or member of the workforce.

What's available

My research focused on the person receiving adult education rather than on the provider, so that information on places of learning, subjects available and methods of teaching came first from the women in my sample. Some further investigation led to the following outline of subjects available in formal and informal adult learning environments in Melbourne today. It is not meant to be an exhaustive listing—handbooks and manuals provide that—nor is it a description of a situation peculiar to this particular large city. It is a means of observing subtle differences which exist nationally and in other parts of the world in approaches to adult education by the various providers.

Universities and colleges of advanced education

Degree and diploma courses in all faculties are open to adult students, but prerequisites in some areas, for example, mathematics and science, debar many mature-age women. Arts courses include studies in languages, history, politics, and the behavioural sciences. Women's studies is generally available as one section of a larger discipline, such as sociology or history, or in some colleges as a postgraduate diploma course. Subject matter is prescribed, although there is the opportunity to choose areas of specific interest within tutorial topics and subjects options.

Colleges of TAFE and institutes of technology

Similar courses as those above are offered, but there is a little more flexibility in student involvement in course design. One particular course in community education was commented upon by a woman during an interview. She said that the lecturer put his theories on community education into practice, requiring the students to develop and evaluate their own courses. This practice may occur in other formal situations, but since I did not attempt to evaluate all adult learning establishments, the extent of the practice of involving students in developing and evaluating their own courses in not known. It would be interesting to investigate this further.

High-school and technical-school day and evening classes

Evening classes offer courses for accreditation at Year 12 level. Subjects offered include English, histories, politics and other humanities subjects, as well as general mathematics, pure and applied mathematics, physics, chemistry, computer science and accounting. I shall discuss the participation of women in subjects other than humanities later, but it is interesting to note here that in a situation where restraints of time caused by paid or unpaid work during the day make evening classes the only avenue for undertaking the desired course of study, it is mostly men who do mathematics and physics. In very small numbers women study accounting and chemistry. This evidence is reinforced by the findings of a recent report on 'Second Chance' education for adults in the Australian Capital Territory.

Some high schools offer a mix of day and evening classes, thus creating options for mature-age students to attend either, and offering more flexibility of timetabling. Mature-age women who attend high-school day classes are free, of course, and to take up the range of courses available at the school, but again, few of them opt for mathematics or sciences. Where schools conduct courses which require a degree of student participation in their course development, the adult woman student has some possibility of meeting her own needs. One teacher, who had interviewed a number of ex-students in this category, said that the negotiating of courses was the aspect they enjoyed most and one which had the most lasting effect on their lives.

Council of Adult Education

English, histories, politics and other humanities up to Year 12 are available at the Council of Adult Education. Group 1 maths and sciences are not widely available but business mathematics can be studied. The council does not have courses at Year 12 in which students can participate in development and assessment; it provides a number of courses preparing for return to study which concentrate on study skills, essay-writing and examination techniques. There may be some improvement in self-confidence in these areas as a result. In fact, I would argue that a thorough preparation in the skills of note-taking, essay-planning and writing and analysis of examination questions not only contributes to the confidence with which the mature-age student approaches her task, but helps to demystify much of the language which is used in lectures, examination questions and essay topics. Prepared in this way, the returning adult student is less likely to blame what she often sees as her own incompetence, stupidity or lack of intelligence when faced with tasks of analysis and writing.

More specifically geared to develop confidence through sharing of experiences is the 'Stepping Stones' program which reflects the commitment of the Council of Adult Education to the education of adult women who may have been disadvantaged by social or economic conditions when they were younger. It provides the opportunity to build self-confidence, to share idea and feelings with other women and to consider the possibility of further study, retraining, employment or voluntary work.

TAFE women's access programs

Women's access programs are those which have been specifically designed to help women who are interested in returning to education and work. Originally they were oriented towards mature women who had had a substantial period of time away from education and/or paid work. But because these programs have now been established in many centres, and in response to a variety of needs, there is considerable variation among them, ranging between those designed for 'personal development', preparation for formal study, and Year 12 classes specifically for women. As one interviewee commented, the Women's Access Program at her local TAFE college consisted entirely of discussion of Year 12 and what it could lead to. There was no mention of study skills required or any of the problems of reorganising of time or coping with family responsibilities that so many women experience. Others have courses such as English for fun, assertiveness training and confidence building, all attempting to meet the needs of women in the community who are uncertain of their abilities. Access to mathematics by way of bridging courses is also available in some women's access programs.

One of the larger inner city institutes of technology offers the opportunity for women and girls who are interested in extending their educational and career options to attend a course where there is extensive counselling, as well as the opportunity to participate in course design, in a supportive and friendly environment. Creche facilities are available and there are no entrance requirements. This activity is similar to the New Opportunities for Women (NOW) courses, operating in New South Wales and at Hartfield Polytechnic in England. They offer a comprehensive guide to mature women who have been out of the labour market for some years and who wish to return to work or study but are unsure of how best to do so. At the institute in Melbourne, a bridging program is offered for women, with courses in personal and communication skills, writing skills, psychology, social studies and preparatory science and mathematics as well as courses in electronics.

Women's access has come to mean many different things. Many providers assume that the decision to come to a course has been preceded by a decision to study in order to return to work. In other situations, formal study has become 'women's access', possibly overlooking the needs of the would-be students whose perceptions of their own abilities are too low to allow them attempt such a course. At other venues, courses are designed to encourage participation and increased confidence in the adult women who enrol.

Women's learning centres

The descriptive name 'women's learning centre' is used in this book to cover the range of similar but sometimes quite different learning environments in which women participate. Other names, such as neighbourhood learning centre, neighbourhood house, community centre or house, living and learning centre or women's cooperative, are used by the many community-based centres which have developed in Australia since 1974. In 1979, an Association of Neighbourhood Learning Centres was established.

Women's learning centres are funded by a variety of government departments on a number of different criteria. TAFE provides funds for the activities of some centres, as well as staff, some of whom teach in local TAFE colleges also. It is impossible, in the absence of a complete central registry of informal learning centres, to find out numbers, nor is it possible to assume that there is a common philosophy based on the needs of women in education. Since my research began with its emphasis on women in formal education, the discovery of the extent of the activities of informal learning centres led me at first to investigate the provision of accredited courses of study in these establishments. When I visited a number of women's learning centres, I realised that, while many of them do provide Year 12 courses for examination and credentials, there are many other important activities and approaches to adult education. For example, subjects like English for fun cater for students who want to study English but who may fear that they will not be able to cope with academic requirements.

There is great variation within these centres, content of courses ranging from exclusively craft skills to personal ones, such as assertiveness training, and preparation for academic subjects for Year 12. In 1985, one neighbourhood centre provided tertiary studies to meet the the needs of its participants for higher education in a non-traditional environment. Developing craft skills are a part of all women's learning centre curricula, with emphases varying from the more functional crafts such as book-binding to the purely decorative, such as cake-decorating. In some cases it is deliberate policy to emphasise the historical and functional worth of crafts such as weaving so that they are not seen as necessarily 'domestic' or 'lesser' activities by the participants. This is part of a philosophy which values traditional women's skills for their importance in our culture rather than placing them in the category of hobby or time-filling activities.

For the most part, the curriculum is devised by a few in response to the requirements of many. A minimal hierarchy is maintained in the interests of order. In some centres there is the opportunity for adult students to become members of the board of management, thus democratising the process of deciding what curriculum is to be offered. Participation by students at a number of suburban women's learning centres in the development of their own Year 12 courses to suit their own aims and objectives is a real attempt to involve adults in assessing their own needs realistically.

On the other hand, many providers follow the traditional route of providing access to formal education, and there is some justification for this. It has been pointed out that 'even a fairly knowledgeable member of the general public . . . would find it difficult to articulate a need for return to education on a broad base that enabled advances to be made without reference to an educational starting point and a qualifying finishing post'. I do not agree entirely. More tentative women find the terms 'women's access' and 'confidence building' more in keeping with the way they view themselves and their potential.

Formal tertiary institutions have little need to advertise their standard courses, although some do explain new or unusual courses in daily newspapers. High and technical schools likewise use very limited advertising, sometimes in local papers, for their formal subjects. The Council of Adult Education has a very comprehensive advertising campaign explaining available courses which is said to reach every house in Melbourne. In all these cases, the prospective student takes the initiative in recognising her perceived educational need and pursues it. For some women, the process is not so straightforward. A coordinator of a women's learning centre in a working-class suburb recounted the situation where a woman had rung the centre after keeping copies of their advertisement for over three years. Her very low self-confidence had stopped her from taking the step to ring the centre, but after a long telephone conversation, she eventually came. As the coordinator remarked, 'The survival instinct is stronger than all other messages'. The coordinator of another centre recorded similar experiences with women who rang first. After making contact with one person, they then visited the centre, had coffee and talked at length with that person before they became confident enough to enrol in a course.

Community centres and women's learning centres use local papers extensively to advertise their presence, although one spokeswoman added that they also doorknocked and circulated questionnaires enquiring what residents would like to learn. This method, she said, broke down criticism by the community that the centre was subversive in some way. Nearly one-third of the questionnaire respondents discovered their place of learning through newspapers, evidence enough that this is an effective way of advertising.

There is a problem that some potential students who may fear such 'feminist' courses as assertiveness training may be alienated. Some centres avoid this by using less provocative names for their courses, such as 'Yes you can!' The uncertainty of a number of adult women students is reflected in this fear of feminism. It is equally feasible that their perceived educational needs are distorted by other ideological pressures of which they are unaware, such as the notion that they should accept total responsibility for child-rearing and domestic organisation, or that pursuing their needs is a selfish action.

The phrasing of some advertisements presupposes that the returner should choose formal study when she first considers her educational needs. For example, an evening-school advertisement asks, 'Thinking of study in 1985?' and claims that the HSC is *still* the key (the emphasis is theirs). There is a danger in this approach if the woman has not really considered why she wants to return to study. It might well be that she decides to pursue a qualification when she understands more fully the influences which are shaping her view of self and her actions. Then she will choose a key that will open the doors to her considered path. It may be a Year 12 or higher credential, or it may not.

'The problem that has no name', as Betty Friedan terms it, may well have its manifestation in personal illness and problems with children, so it would seem obvious that women's learning centres and other local venues for learning should advertise in doctor's surgeries and community health centres, as well as in libraries, preschool centres, primary and secondary schools, supermarket notice boards and shop windows. When catering for perceived needs as well as for those that underlie them, advertising is a very subtle aspect of women's education.

Perhaps the most unifying aspect of the education available for women is the fact that except in tertiary institutions and high and technical schools, it is mostly for women only, despite the fact that in Victoria it is illegal for an education institution which offers courses for both sexes to refuse an enrolment on the grounds of sex. Commenting on the problem of excluding men from a district cooperative, the coordinator said that there had been no decision to disallow men, but there had been a decision to offer courses and advertise in such a way to attract women only because if men joined the group, women would automatically step back and let them organise. The management committee thought that if women were forced to do things by themselves they would grow in confidence and in competence.

The Council of Adult Education, at the time of my research, was offering 26 women's issues courses as well as 'women's days' at a cost of $34, where a variety of workshops relating to women's sexuality, workforce participation, women and the media and marriage were available. These non-accredited courses are similar in content to many of those offered in women's learning centres, but differ in that there is little or no continuity, and therefore little opportunity to form bonds or networks which are such an important aspect of the women's learning centre philosophy. Factors such as location of classes and means of travelling exacerbate the problem of forming lasting networks as a result of these classes.

Subjects and courses

The provision of mainly humanities subjects as well as the daytime programming of classes especially for women reinforces the assumption that they freely choose both the subjects to be studied and the times when they will participate. They do choose, but most often because they accept without question those internalised values about their capacities and their responsibilities. Sometimes the 'free choice' is in fact completely dictated by the demands of the family, as Claire, a 50-year-old arts student suggested:

★ I found this was the case with many of the women at university. I chose my subjects to fit in with times when I could afford to be away from home.

Beatrice, a divorcee with two children, about to start an arts course, said that she would do anything that fitted in between 9 am and 3 pm. Many women like Claire and Beatrice help to perpetuate the assumption upon which much adult education for women is organised, that is, that it must take place while their children are at school.

There is a Catch-22 here, of course, in that, in purely practical terms, this is the time when many women are relatively free of time constraints. More than one-third of the questionnaire respondents chose times of classes for this reason. Nevertheless, when you consider that most adult women attend classes part-time and that fitting in with the demands of family is the main reason for choosing daytime classes, the fact that certain subjects are timetabled between 9 am and 3 pm has considerable influence on the choices that can be made. If English and the humanities are the subjects most readily available at these times she is likely to accept these traditionally 'feminine' choices without question for practical reasons as well as for notions of her own ability which have been internalised. If maths, sciences, accounting and business studies are available only in the late afternoon or evening, it is only extremely determined and well-supported women who will be able to make the necessary arrangements to attend classes in them.

A brief look at the development of daytime classes in the Council of Adult Education reveals that the assumption of women's priorities of time, together with those relating to their perceived needs, influenced both the establishment of such classes and the subject matter they would contain. Until 1964, almost all classes were conducted in the evening. A large number of married women enrolled in these evening classes and, having proved their interest in adult education, daytime classes were set up in that year. They provided tuition in non-vocational subjects and languages, and in 1966 a course entitled 'The Changing Role of Women' was introduced at the city as well as at a suburban centre.

By 1969, daytime classes for married women had been set up to prepare them for the matriculation examination. Among the main factors influencing this innovation was the recognition that married women had specific timetabling requirements. Classes were scheduled between 10 am and 2.30 pm and no meetings were programmed during the school holidays. Enrolments were restricted to those who were eligible to prepare for the matriculation examination and who were aged between 23 and 35 years. Subjects offered were English expression, literature, social studies, Australian history, eighteenth-century history, geography, French and German. German and geography were cancelled through lack of support and the French enrolment just reached the minimum of fifteen.

In 1971-72 daytime classes were opened in the suburbs and the venues were extended in the following year, but not to the northern or western suburbs because of difficulty of staffing and lack of demand in those areas. General maths was included in that year. In 1982, 220 women and 24 men over the age of 25 who attended council classes presented for HSC examinations, two men for general mathematics, one man for computer science, but no women attempted examinations in these subjects. The only subject which could possibly be seen as not a traditional one for women, accounting, was taken by five women and three men.

There is a similar pattern of little or no participation by women over 25 in high- or technical-school evening classes in mathematics, physics and chemistry, but some participation in accounting. Further investigations would be needed to determine whether more women would take these subjects if they were available during the day. The ACT study to which I referred earlier also found that women seldom take maths and science. This lack of participation could be used as an argument for not providing these subjects in daytime classes mainly attended by women, or even exclusively set up for women. The fact remains, however, that unless they are made available, women will not see them as within their capabilities. The problem of meeting needs, or of creating them, is a complex one. I mention the timetabling and the range of subjects at secondary level that are offered specifically for women by the Council of Adult Education and women's learning centres simply to have the reader reflect on something that might otherwise have been taken for granted. These organisations provide invaluable experiences for women when they first return to study. In fact, one woman thanked the local women's learning centre most heartily:

★ For many years I considered night school, but as my husband could not always be home in time to start at 6 pm I kept postponing it. Also morning classes are more enjoyable as one is not so tired.

I have also noticed that women's learning centres seldom include maths or science subjects in their courses, unless at an introductory level. If an adult student wishes to continue with these subjects after the introductory classes, she must go on to a high-school day or evening class. In a day class, it is likely that she would be a lone adult in a class of mainly adolescent boys. The viability of offering science classes in informal environments was discussed with several coordinators of women's learning centres who agreed that cost of equipment was the chief restraint.

The subjects women choose

The subjects being studied give an indication of the view of one's own capability and perceived needs as well as a reflection of the provider's understanding of the needs, and possibly the capabilities, of prospective students. I have made a summary of the subjects that were being studied by the women in the sample at the time when I collected the data, or that had been studied during their education as adults (see Table 5 in the Appendix).

The large number of mature-age students who study English and/or English literature is understandable in the light of the generally accepted assumption that women are good at literary subjects, and for many women English is the least intimidating of the formal subjects offered. As one adult student commented, 'You can try the water with English. If you can't cope, there is nothing lost.'

Apart from revealing the very tentative and rather negative approach which other studies in Australia and England have also found as typifying the mature-age woman student, this comment reveals the comfort the adult woman feels in taking a subject she pursued in her youth, especially when she feels unsure about her abilities. The study of English and English literature can be viewed as an extension of study in a book group and which therefore can be dismissed as a hobby if it proves too difficult, or if the mature-age student is challenged by family or friends about her priorities in using her time.

The popularity of history and other subjects which deal with human actions and relations, such as psychology, sociology, human development and society supports the notion that women are naturally interested in the humanities at the expense of mathematics and sciences. Two-thirds of the women in the sample said that they chose subjects out of interest. This situation supports the theory that women study arts because of a social definition of feminine qualities and inabilities, such as concern for humanity and fear of all things technical. By accepting this definition without examining the enormous ramifications of it, for example, that men are not so concerned with humanity and that women are unable to cope with technology, they themselves contribute to perpetuating this image. Making a choice to study arts *after* examination and understanding of this situation is quite a different matter. Awareness of social pressures such as this could also help to break down stereotypes of men's needs and abilities, particularly when one considers the influence of a mother on the attitudes of her sons. Although there are a small number of tertiary institutions trying to interest women in non-traditional courses, formal education rarely challenges the assumptions that women have about appropriate career choices, nor does it deliberately challenge the criteria by which their position in the unpaid workforce is given such a low status. The small percentage of the sample who were studying or had studied mathematics, and science (including biology), reinforces the claim that many women accept a social definition of their needs and abilities, but it also highlights another aspect of the provision of adult education: mathematics, physics and chemistry are rarely available to day students at secondary level unless they attend high school classes.

In the interviews, subjects were discussed for the interest of their content to the individual, and the method of dealing with the subject matter in class. For example, one woman who lives in a suburb which has a large number of Greek inhabitants remarked that her understanding of these people had grown tremendously through the class discussion of the novels in the 'cultural conflict' section of HSC English and she has become much more tolerant. Another found that her understanding of women and their place in the world increased when she took the women's study option for the writing workshop section of HSC English, a project that required individual research and reading under the direction of the teacher. A comment on a questionnaire pinpointed the change in herself that one women could see. She said,

★ My growth, when I look back, has been tremendous and doing women's studies in sociology has really strengthened how I had become to feel—an individual. I now make a point of having friends outside the 'couple' relationship and go on regular outings with them to films or dinner—things I would have felt guilty about prior to study (on a regular basis I mean).

The sheer numbers of women who were studying or had studied English or English literature, together with the subject matter itself, suggest that these subjects have the potential to become a vehicle for group discussion, self-reflection, and personal change in view of self and society. But the methods of handling the subject matter, that is, the skills of the teacher in fostering group dynamics and drawing on the life experiences of the adult students, are essential contributions to the process. If the student's main focus is on the credential at the end of the course, the content often becomes something to be mastered, rather than a means of exploring the world and one's view of it. Adult students who see self-development as a reason to return to study should consider this point because, while they most likely will feel some satisfaction in gaining a credential, it does not necessarily follow that they will develop their own perspectives unless there is time in their own timetable and in the learning situation to explore the content of courses fully.

There are a number of subjects which have the potential to challenge the world view of the mature-age student. One women said that she had become a little more cynical about the world around her especially since studying sociology. A study of classical civilisation provided another with a new understanding of the position and power of women in antiquity. Of her learning situation, she commented:

★ At the Co-op [learning centre] groups get together and talk. Women see that the media and the political structure push them into a role (I'm not talking about the feminist movement) and group support creates change.

The option entitled 'Women' in the Australian history course was the source of support for attitudes which had already begun to change for Jenny, a 27-year-old single mother, who was studying HSC first at a high-school evening class then as a day student in a high-school. The teaching Jenny received was quite formal, with little opportunity for group discussion, particularly as she was the only mature-age student in the day class. It was a traumatic personal experience that left her with the resolve to 'be in control of her own life', and the content of her study, particularly the Australian history option, provided vicarious support through her empathy with the experiences of many women in Australian history.

By contrast to Jenny's learning environment, Moira studied politics at a high-school evening class as well as at a women's learning centre because she thought her male teacher at the centre was not giving the class enough information to prepare for an HSC examination. Her reflection on her learning process provides an insight into how adults learn which is very revealing:

★ Politics classes at the House make me think about relations, whereas facts and figures that I thought were important are really abstract. How does it affect me in my daily life? This was the question at the House and because there was no hierarchy, you were not afraid of being wrong. I found I was learning quite a lot.

A change in attitude to men was the direct result of subject content according to two interviewees. Lena studied psychology and sociology in her arts degree and found herself questioning the fact that she deferred to her husband in almost all decisions. She now values her own opinions. Betty, through a study of the subject, human development and society at HSC level, now speaks her mind, whereas previously she 'honestly believed that what men said was valid and should be accepted'. In her preparation for a business studies degree, Penelope found that the content of the industrial relations course was rewarding for her:

★ It was basically human resource development and social relations, subjects that made me think about myself and my position in the world.

She received encouragement in her first year from teachers who gave her good marks and comments on her work, but fostering group discussion was not a specific teaching method.

Some subject matter has the power to stimulate a degree of self-reflection, as the experiences of Jenny, Lena and Penelope suggest, provided that preparing for examination does not demand too much time and that the mature-age student sees the connections between the subject matter and her own experience. Some subjects, particularly maths and science, and some students, require the skills of a teacher to bring about the situation where she will make the abstract material relate to personal experience. The teacher might raise questions which evoke a personal response, or she might facilitate group discussion which links individual experiences with the subject matter, thus personalising the learning.

Another important factor in openness to change is the stage of the adult's life at which she is studying. For example, Jenny, Lena and Penelope had each suffered personal trauma before they returned to study. Presumably this had made them already open to change and the subject matter was sufficient in itself to prompt a degree of self-reflection. This connection was not explored specifically because these very personal revelations were offered to me in strict confidence after lengthy discussion on other aspects of returning to study. But it does suggest that if the teacher is not trained to use subject matter as a means of stimulating self-reflection, such a reaction is entirely dependent on the sensitivity of the mature-age student to it, or the timing of her return to study in relation to important life experiences.

Women's studies

There are two or three reasons why such a small number of women in the sample were taking women's studies. When this data was gathered, women's studies was not available as an HSC subject, so that women selecting subjects would have chosen from those most commonly available at adult education venues. Women who did study this subject were those who attended women's learning centres, where it was non-accredited, or universities or colleges where it was either an option in a course, or a postgraduate diploma course. The choice then displays a definite interest in or commitment to the position of women in society which is not generally shared by most mature-age women students in places of formal education. As well as this, a fear of being labelled 'feminist' would inhibit some women from choosing the subject.

There are also practical problems in setting up women's studies programs. Reports from teachers and researchers suggest that this subject does not fit easily into a system where students expect to be assessed for credentials. While women are very glad of a chance to talk freely in an open way and to set up support systems for themselves and other women, this is difficult if the course is subject to external validation. This situation raises the problem of establishing a learning environment which is supportive and in which experiences are shared in the midst of a wider community acceptance of competition and examinations in education. It has been argued that women's studies courses can actually disrupt solidarity between women students when they are competing in a formal course for accreditation. In other words, there is an attempt to serve two masters: one which prescribes competition and achievement as a means by which women can change their lives, and the other which tries to value each person and her contribution to the shared experiences of the group in an uncompetitive environment.

A New Zealand study claims that the specifically personal orientation of courses related to women's studies, such as assertiveness training, without an analysis of women in society, negates any possibility of their contributing to broad social change. The comments of an interviewee who attended a brief assertiveness training course at a women's learning centre support this claim. She told me that she tried to be more assertive at home, but her family did not like her that way. Instead of arguing about her children's responsibilities for household chores, she simply closed the door and went out to work as a library technician, but she was not prepared to challenge them enough to effect any change in her family's attitudes to sharing household responsibilities.

It seems likely that, while women's studies courses, whether taught in an academic or an informal environment, may be ideal for developing discussions, many other subjects can be treated in a way which allows for similar personalisation of learning, and for a woman's perspective to be brought to their analysis and interpretation. The important element is the development of a supportive and stimulating group where experiences are shared and issues discussed. While it could be argued that a more assertive, confident woman will bring about changes in her own life and in her family that will eventually have repercussions in the wider society, such progress can be hindered or aborted by pressure inflicted on the individual. If she does not continue to have support of a group after the class finishes, she is thrown on her own resources, possibly without an understanding of the influences of social forces on her feeling and actions. If involvement with the learning environment extends over a length of time, allowing for the discussion of a variety of issues relating to society in a friendly, supportive atmosphere, the student will be helped in two ways: she will have learned to think about her personal experiences in a wider context and she will have the confidence and the analytical skills to explain her attitudes and actions, if necessary, at work or with her friends.

From observation and discussion with teachers and adult students in five women's learning centres, I maintain that, provided the subject matter and the teaching methods combine to alert the student to her position in the structure of society, her decision to continue within the education system or to choose less formal methods of satisfying her desire for learning is unimportant. As long as she knows why she is studying, she is not labouring under the illusion that education will, in itself, free her from depression, or from a feeling of inadequacy and low self-worth. In other words, an understanding of the principal economic and cultural ideologies of our society should ideally precede the decision to take on formal study. Such understanding may then contribute to a gradual reassessment of ability to pursue science or commerce, creating a change in the provision of these subjects for women who choose to study during the day.

This argument has been carried even further in the contention that even classes in cookery and fashioncrafts should include an analysis of the dynamics of the cultural/class basis, raising questions about why women respond to fashions and the economics of producing and marketing them. The emphasis again is on encouraging thinking and reflection rather than acceptance of a body of knowledge or skills. Good teachers do this as a matter of course, but the circumstances often detract from the impact on the student. Shortage of time, preparation for examination or the lack of a supportive group in which to discuss, analyse and personalise the material all contribute to the possibility of acceptance without reflection. I feel very strongly that it is important that, having learned to reflect on such aspects of her thinking, the adult student should feel confident enough to accept or reject the underlying social assumptions about her abilities and educational needs. In this way she is acting as autonomously as any individual who lives in society can be expected to act.

I stress the paradox of providing preparation for examinations, which is a highly competitive activity, while at the same time trying to create a sharing learning environment. If, however, the preparation for formal examinations also incorporates in the teaching method a sharing of experiences and discussion regarding social structures and ideologies, and time is not a pressing factor in gaining the credential, such a course of study may serve these two purposes. Much depends on the teacher and the philosophy of the institution providing the courses.

Times of classes: five women who defied tradition

The problems which confront women who wish to pursue courses other than those available during the day and as part-time students are highlighted in the following examples. There is considerable rigidity in the underlying assumptions held by some tertiary institutions about class timetabling.

Sarah, who is married with three children, was studying accountancy at an institute of technology at the time of our conversation. She admitted that childcare created a big financial strain on her husband's resources, but, because she means to pursue a career as soon as she is qualified, he viewed it as an investment. She dropped out of the first year statistics class for two reasons. The male teacher asked whether she had a child. When she answered yes, he said, 'Well, you won't last'. This unsupportive attitude, together with the difficulty of coping with maths, proved him correct. The other reason was that classes were between 7.30 pm and 9.30 pm. Despite the difficulty of coping with family responsibilities and times of classes, she returned the next year with a different lecturer and passed the subject. The rigidity of the institutional structure worked against her in that, as a part-time student, classes were available only at night unless the student was on day release, usually from a government department, and then there were only limited places available. Only after achieving exceptionally well in first year subjects was she able to negotiate with the institution to attend day classes. This evidence supports the argument that much higher education has grown up as a handmaiden of employment. In this case, it was prescribed that part-time students must occupy only evening classes, presumably after the student had finished the day's paid work. The adult woman student, it seems, has the choice of attempting full-time study as well as looking after her family, or attending night classes from 5.30 pm until 9.30 pm, the most demanding time when attending to young children.

Rita, aged 32, divorced with two children, had been forced to drop out of her chosen course because of timetabling. The graduate degree in psychology at a college of TAFE in which she enrolled required that she attend lectures twice a week between 5 pm and 9 pm and tutorials twice a week between 2 pm and 5 pm. Without childcare facilities, or the financial ability to provide them herself, she gave up the course, but intends to re-enrol in another at a similar level in which she is not particularly interested, simply because the hours are more workable. Between 6 pm and 9 pm she can manage to get to lectures because, by that time, her mother is home from work and can mind the children. The student made an aside about the male day-release students she encountered. She maintained that they contributed little to classes and generally discussions were dry and boring as a result, perhaps a reflection of the lack of interest often shown when study is primarily for the purpose of credentials and promotion.

June, aged 39, married with three children, was taking a graduate diploma in health education at a college of advanced education and had to attend two nights a week between 5 pm and 8 pm. Her children were quite antagonistic, and even used her absence as an excuse for not having homework done. This made her feel guilty and undermined her pleasure in studying something that interested her, and for which her nursing training was an asset.

Peg, aged 40, with two children, was majoring in psychology at a TAFE college where the psychology lecture was between 5 pm and 6 pm. No children were allowed in the lectures, and it was too early to expect her husband to be home to mind the children, so she was forced to employ a baby-sitter, although her financial situation did not really allow it.

Pamela, a 39-year-old science student, married with three children, compared the science timetable with that of arts and concluded that it was much more difficult for a mother to do a science degree than an arts degree. She had to attend university every day because psychology had four lectures and one practical session per week. She made the point that, even as a part-time student, she had no days that were not taken up with study. She became involved with the creche cooperative at her university and set up a network of support both at the university and in her neighbourhood which she claimed was essential. She also made another interesting point about the intensity of the course, which may be only tangentially related to times of classes, but which gives some insight into restrictions of time in relation to the potential of adult education for change:

★ It's a rat race. There are quotas for everything and if you don't get the marks, you don't get in. So you have to get good marks to do what you want to do in the Science Faculty.

A mature-age student working under stress of that kind would have little chance of achieving her aims if she also had to cope with apathy or antagonism from her husband or children. As Pamela pointed out, 'If your husband is against you, you might as well get divorced straightaway or give up'.

I have previously mentioned that in arranging timetables to suit the mature-age woman student, there is a dilemma. If they are arranged around school times, the present expectation that women's priorities of time should be so ordered is not challenged, nor are her choices of subjects if they also fulfil the expectation that women will want to study the humanities rather than subjects with a maths, science or commerce component. If they are not arranged around school timetables in a deliberate attempt to break down these priorities (a situation not discovered in my research or my reading of the literature), or if they are arranged to suit the single person who is employed during the day and with no family commitments, the mature-age women with family commitments has to be exceptionally motivated, extremely well supported by her family, or well enough off to pay for expensive childcare to make the effort to overcome this difficulty. If she is tentative about her aims, or even if she becomes firm in her direction after preliminary experience, discussion and counselling, the obstacles to her choosing non-traditional subjects in out-of-school hours are still great.

It would be unrealistic to suggest that the tertiary education system should present an ideal situation for the woman student with family commitments. The needs of full-time paid workers who wish to study must be accommodated. Fitting in with family commitments, however, places limits on the times available for attending classes which are just as restricting as paid work. For this reason tertiary institutions should be flexible in allowing places in all classes for those whose hours of work, paid or unpaid, restrict their access to them.

Childcare

Adequate and cheap childcare is essential if women are to participate in adult education, whether at the informal, non-accredited level, or at undergraduate or postgraduate level. The politics of funding, Health Department regulations and the means by which some establishments circumvent the bureaucratic edicts on childcare are too complex to deal with in this book. However, in the context of the encouragement and restraints under which mature-age women return to study, and in which they are encouraged or otherwise to change the view of themselves and their abilities, it is fitting to discuss provision of this important service. Lack of childcare in any institution of learning tacitly accepts the notion that women with young children should automatically be excluded unless they are in the financial position to pay for private childcare. Not only does this assumption reflect on the institution itself, it contributes to the maintenance of the view that women bear prime responsibility for young children, one which, in turn, perpetuates the burden of guilt of which so many mature-age women students speak. In other words, lack of good-quality childcare is part of a circle which keeps women at a disadvantage and helpless to redress it. A comment from a woman at a learning centre makes this point:

★ Cheap childminding is necessary for many women as when study is viewed as a frivolous luxury, the money spent in often strained financial circumstances can make the difference between study or home duties.

While over a third of the women in my sample chose daytime classes because the children were at school, a small number did so because childcare was provided for their preschool children. Julie, a past student and administrator at a women's learning centre, said that the childcare facilities took precedence for many young women over the actual educational activities offered. In other words, their desire to make social contact in a learning environment where, at the same time, their children could be close by and adequately cared for, was the motivating force behind their educational venture. In the words of Marion,

★ The creche is the central part of the Co-op. There would not be so many women there without it.

At the same women's learning centre, women who could not afford fees for classes could work in childminding, or as class secretaries, in lieu of fees. Whether they participated in craft or academic activities, or moved from one to the other, their initial step into learning was through their work in the creche. It was reported that the availability of childcare led to such a demand for HSC English classes that prospective students formed queues from early morning on enrolment days. The socially levelling influence of participation in childcare can be seen in Alison's comment:

★ In childminding you see people and know they are just like you. They often come because of the creche and finish up doing secondary-level courses.

A single mother, at present at university doing an arts degree, said that she could not have begun without the childminding provided at the women's learning centre which she previously attended.

The quality of childcare is, of course, important to all mothers. An interviewee at an outer suburban women's learning centre commented that, besides the importance of not using the unpaid time of someone else (a friend or relation) while attending classes, quality childcare with people who become familiar to the children is a valuable experience for the children themselves. It can also be the deciding factor for some women, as another learning centre student pointed out.

Visits to five women's learning centres and literature on many others confirmed that the provision of inexpensive childcare on the premises was considered a fundamental right. Some Council of Adult Education centres now provide childcare, and TAFE colleges where women's access programs are conducted consider it a necessity, but high schools which conduct Year 12 classes during the day or in the evening rarely have this facility. In most tertiary institutions, childcare is scarce and sometimes expensive.

If childcare during school holidays is undertaken as a personal, rather than a public, responsibility the adult woman student can still be disadvantaged. Marie's primary concern for the care of her children during school holidays worked against her when she applied for enrolment in a city institute of technology. She asked the interviewer whether term breaks coincided with school holidays. His reply was that they wanted people with commitment to the course. She did not get in.

Fees

In 1974-75, with the introduction of federal government grants to subsidise adult students full-time for the HSC, more subjects and more venues in the northern suburbs were made available by the Council of Adult Education. This suggests that payment of fees is in itself an inhibiting factor for many mature-age women students, particularly those in less affluent socioeconomic circumstances. One women told me of her concern:

★ Financial problems have been a major worry as I often feel guilty about going to school when I know I could or perhaps should be working. Although I have been more fortunate than most in my class at the Co-op, as, being class secretary, my fees are paid, I'm still left in a position where I have to borrow books, which makes study with researching most difficult.

As three of the interviewees intimated, even in middle-class suburbs it cannot be assumed that the adult woman has money to spend freely on her own education.

A college of TAFE which serves a mainly working-class area advertised a personal development course, including assertiveness skills and self-esteem, at $69 for two and a half days and $38 for one day. This is surely a prohibitive amount, requiring considerable assertiveness and sense of self-worth to justify the extraction of such an amount from the family income.

A woman who had been one of a group at a women's learning centre had gained entry to a university through her adult studies at the centre but had deferred because of costs such as union fees, books and travel. Her family commitments prohibited her from undertaking full-time study by which she may have been eligible for the TEAS (now Austudy) allowance, so she returned to the learning centre for more classes at Year 12 level. Having gained a sense of self-worth through her involvement with the centre, she had chosen to go further with her education to pursue a career, but lack of money forced her to abandon that plan. Some women's learning centres have means by which those who cannot afford fees can work in childcare or as class secretary in lieu of fees, but, as noted in one such centre, many women cannot tolerate the embarrassment of being seen to be in this position when they first join the acitivities of the centre.

Costs of courses at all levels, including books and travel, are important when discussing access to adult education. There is some irony in the cycle: if a woman does not have a high enough sense of her own worth to claim a share of the family income for her personal development, or if she would suffer guilt as a result, she will never be in a position to improve her self-image, whether by the method of meeting socially constructed measurements of worth such as credentials, or by attending personal development courses such as those advertised by some TAFE colleges. In this context, it is obvious how the imposition of administration fees for part-time and full-time students badly affects the chances of women to further their educations. More than that, it subtly reinforces the assumption that many women themselves hold, that their own needs for self-development through education are not as important as those of other family members. Only through government financial assistance for the needy part-time adult student at secondary and tertiary levels can this cycle be broken.

Counselling

★ When the adult student is uncertain about her expectations of her return to study, she is in doubt about what she should aim at—future employment, continuation of higher education or what?

The dilemma experienced by many mature-age students when they are faced with the plethora of subject possibilities, even within the humanities, but with different entry requirements, was mentioned by many of the women in my sample. One HSC student said she had no idea what was available or where to go for it when she went to a high-school evening class. Another woman said she just enrolled for the first thing she saw. She found that in the class in which she enrolled there were mainly young people under 21 and she found her experience a very lonely one. The problem of choices is even more complex at university, according to three of the interviewees, who felt overwhelmed by the subject choices and sequences of units on which they had to make decisions. Each felt she had made an ad hoc decision, without really understanding what the ramifications might be.

Tertiary and some secondary institutions provide student counselling services, but as one mature-age student pointed out, she had to 'forget all her qualms about going to a counsellor' before she could bring herself to do it. Counselling had connotations of psychological disorders for some older students, and, in the formal setting of a university, the counsellor is sometimes seen to be unapproachable. A 48-year-old interviewee commented:

★ I was brought up in the old school where you never asked for help. You always managed by yourself.

Such a stoic attitude pervades many of the comments, almost as if the act of returning to study is seen as a test of personal strength and endurance against difficult odds, in which seeking counselling would represent a personal weakness.

Some counsellors see their brief as helping with essay-writing skills and other areas of study which students find difficult. A conversation with the coordinator of a suburban high-school evening school suggested this view of counselling. He was eager to point out that other schools in the area providing evening classes for the HSC did not have the services of a counsellor at all. Practical help is, of course, essential, but there are some less obvious areas in which support is required. The coordinator of the above school was aware of social pressures suffered by some adult women students as he reported that a number of them dropped out of courses because they were ridiculed by their family and peers. Counselling in a supportive situation in which social pressures are discussed and understood is necessary if the dropout rate is to be arrested. Even for those women who battle on despite negative reactions from family and friends, personal growth can only be assured if guilt is removed and personal sense of worth is established.

Expert advice in choosing subjects is only one aspect of counselling, and a number of tertiary institutions and researchers are aware of this. It is generally agreed that mature-age applicants to universities and colleges of advanced education should be made aware of what is at issue in any decision to enrol in tertiary courses. Such a 'warning' might well deter the less confident mature-age woman student altogether.

In the 1973-74 annual report of the Council of Adult Education it was noted that the dropout rate among mature-age women preparing for HSC examinations was high, and as a possible solution to this problem a summer school was established to provide introductory courses, which 'particularly helped house-wives who returned to study'. In the same report it was noted that the dropout rate at a newly opened learning exchange was almost nil because of the informal environment where coffee was served and discussion was held in tutorial groups. The difference in approach to the perceived needs or problems of adult women students is epitomised in the summer school on the one hand and the informal learning environment on the other. The provision of extra, remedial or preparatory courses is based on the belief that help is needed to bridge the gap between previous and present education, and that improved skills and therefore better results will offset dropout rates. The bridging of this gap is certainly important as a large number of women pointed out. But other problems, such as disparagement of efforts or low self-image affecting performance, must also be addressed.

It is fitting to discuss counselling adult women students in the context of the distinction posed at the beginning of this chapter. Education and learning are concepts which many of us see as synonymous when we return to study, so clarification of the difference in the initial stages would surely be worthwhile. It is possible that education can take place without challenge to the ideas of the student. It is 'out there'—it improves general knowledge and skills but it is remote from the circle in which you live. With greatly improved knowledge of historical events and literature, the adult woman is a more interesting person, but new-found confidence is often undermined by guilt, the source of which is often not thoroughly understood. A great deal of learning has taken place about society, particularly as she is most likely to be studying the humanities, but only in certain circumstances does she see how these events and ways of thinking have influenced her. Learning then is an activity which requires personal involvement with the subject material. Even mathematical and scientific problems can be approached in this way if the examples are related to the experience of the learner. The next step is to learn skills of analysis including the questioning of assumptions which underlie the points of view presented in an argument. If this skill is deliberately fostered as one which should be carried over into examining personal circumstances, then what might have been seen as a personal, isolated problem can be seen in its wider social context. If counselling before returning to study could take this form, it would clarify reasons and expectations, lead to a more considered choice of subjects, or direct the woman to another path altogether to satisfy her needs.

An effective method would be to conduct a number of social awareness courses in informal environments before enrolment so that the prospective student could then determine her reasons for undertaking study, her methods of coping with pressures from family and friends, and plan her priorities of time to make use of the educational environment which she is entering. Some colleges do have pre-enrolment seminars of this type, with varying emphases on the expectations of students and the pressures, academic and social, with which they have to cope.

These social awareness courses may not have the scope or the environment in which the adult student could fully understand her position in the social structure, but they do at least raise some important questions. They may not produce any significant change in self-image, but an understanding of the hidden reasons why she is undertaking study, for example, low self-image or isolation, and the recognition of the pressures which create a feeling of guilt, would help the student to choose her course of action more critically. These courses would also make the mature-age student aware that she is not alone, an important understanding in coping with any aspects of change.

Social pressures and expectations known to affect women's learning can be addressed even when the subject matter is not directly related to these concerns, and when the potential student is highly motivated to gain a credential. This method uses not so much the skill-development approach but one based on the incorporation of the individual into a group where her ideas and experiences are valued and used in relation to the subject under discussion. Such a teaching method incorporates a degree of counselling in that each person is encouraged to view her own experiences as part of the way in which our society functions. Whether she wishes to pursue a career or study an area of interest at a higher level the adult woman student would have to accept as a circumstance of such study its competitive and relatively isolated conditions. A number of women in my sample who are at present in tertiary institutions have maintained links with women's groups with which they were previously involved. One postgraduate student found contact with the women's learning centre with which she was closely associated to be necessary for renewal of her confidence and purpose. Three of these women expressed disillusion with tertiary education and spoke of giving it up in favour of closer involvement in community education.

The point I stress is that an important aspect of counselling is to suggest the validity of accepting or *rejecting* certain expectations about the value of formal higher education. These include notions about education and status and education leading to paid work. A report on a 'Fresh Horizons' program for adults in metropolitan London made the similar point that 'in a situation that gave time for motives and aspirations to become clearer, for alternatives to be explored and, because it was a context in which growth was taking place, new skills and confidence could be developed. Not the least advantage [of counselling] was that students could decide *not* to embark on new ventures.'

Physical environments for teaching and learning

Universities, colleges of advanced education, institutes of technology, high and technical schools generally provide a physical environment for learning which is in keeping with the traditional, hierarchical structure where the teacher lectures and the student listens. Classrooms and lecture theatres with furniture arrangements to suit a lecture situation are commonly provided. The distancing of the teacher, together with the assumption that he or she has a 'parcel of knowledge' to deliver, perpetuates the view that education is a consumer product. While the atmosphere of a tutorial, often conducted in a small room or office, or the rearrangement of furniture in a high-school evening class may break down formality to some extent, the occasions when teacher and adult student can speak in an atmosphere conducive to any sort of reflection on life experiences in relation to the subject matter are rare. The Council of Adult Education are obviously aware of this problem, particularly in their 'Stepping Stones' and other women's courses, and, like TAFE colleges which provide women's access programs, try to break down the formality of the environments in which they function.

A very important aspect of learning for adult women, that is, the sharing of experiences within a group, is not easily attained in a formal environment for two reasons: the age difference in a group which does not share the common bond of adult womanhood may be so great that older students may be seen by school-age students to be relating their experiences historically, rather than sharing them as experiences common to all group members. Second, the pressure of examination preparation may be too inhibiting. Two interviewees, both undertaking arts degrees, recounted experiences in tutorials where they felt the need to restrain themselves in discussion for fear of appearing too overwhelming in a group of younger students. Another woman said she became guarded about expressing opinions and therefore alienating younger students. A woman in her middle forties who was studying for the HSC commented on the problem of age difference and how she resolved it.

★ Being at a high school among the kids I think I felt my failures more, and sometimes I felt very inadequate among them. I definitely felt the generation gap. However, since attending the Council of Adult Education classes, I feel at ease among people of my own age.

Five women from working-class suburbs of Melbourne who had attended high-school evening classes because they were the only ones available each felt the need to talk to other women of their own age about the subject matter and other experiences concerned with returning to study. One was befriended by the librarian, another developed a friendship by telephone with a mature-age student from the evening class, while two others, a 32-year-old mother of two, and a mother of six in her late forties, felt like 'geriatrics' in a class where most of the students were 21 or younger, and unwilling to become involved in answering questions or discussion. The eagerness of mature-age women to throw themselves into their studies is sometimes a puzzle to younger students. An interviewee in her late forties who was studying fine arts at a college of advanced education observed:

★ Mature-age students are continually accused of working too hard, but I really appreciated all that time to spend on myself. I enjoyed the company of the younger students but there was always a barrier, a generation gap.

Of course, it is not suggested that all adult learning be segregated, but it is important that in their initial return to the learning environment, women should be in a situation to develop the critical awareness of social structures and pressures so that they can more adequately deal with them in higher education, if this is what they ultimately choose.

Informal learning centres for women concentrate on a physical environment which breaks down any suggestion of distance between teachers and students or between women of different ages. They are generally attended by those who live nearby who often have small children and no private transport. All but two interviewees who attended women's learning centres remarked on the advantage of proximity to home and availability of childcare. These two women from a less advantaged suburb said that the learning centre was on public transport and therefore accessible for them during the day, even though it was some distance from their homes. The availability of tertiary education which is equally accessible to them is another matter, although the recent development of a TAFE college in the area should help to ameliorate the position. In a building with rooms furnished with comfortable chairs, with childcare facilities nearby and coffee and food available, an atmosphere is developed which is very conducive to free and open discussion. Many institutions provide rooms for making coffee and relaxing which are specifically for mature-age women students, and support groups often result from the use of these facilities, but there is a sense in which these are a place to run away to, both from the place of learning and the stresses that studying and coping with a family invariably bring. When an informal environment is *also* the place where learning takes place, the adult woman is not caught between two worlds, one where she learns, and the other where she comes for support. Her energies are less divided, particularly as she usually has little distance to travel to a neighbourhood learning centre and she can bring her children if necessary. Granted, these informal places of learning do not cater for those seeking tertiary education, although one centre broke new ground here in 1985, but even for the woman who attained a high level of education while still at school, or even at tertiary level before her return to study as an adult, the subject areas covered and the degree of discussion and debate encountered makes these places of discussion and learning an attractive starting point from which to make decisions about plans for further education or work.

Attitudes of students and teachers to learning

I have found that adult women have varying expectations of being a student again and about what and how they will learn. Some find it hard to make the transition from the way in which they were taught when they were young. Being expected to have an opinion and be able to voice it is often a source of concern. Likewise, as we can see from interviewees' references to teachers and from other literature on adult education, teachers vary in their approaches to adult students. For example, the following excerpts from interviews show two different perceptions of learning by adult students:

★ I had learned a lot, but not one bit of it had affected me personally. I came back to find out more about myself.

By contrast,

★ It's exciting how information slots into some piece of already acquired knowledge.

While the first student expected knowledge that she could use to understand more about herself, the second appears to see herself distanced from a body of knowledge, slotting pieces into a giant jigsaw which is predesigned and limited by its set boundaries.

The sense of control over knowledge is an important aspect of adult learning. It has been argued by Michael Young that when curriculum is accepted as a given, as something not to be questioned, it takes on a life of its own and obscures the human relations in which it, as any conception of knowledge, is embedded.

The result is that education is neither understandable nor controllable by those who use it. An attempt to redress this situation in formal education where subject matter is decided by a body which does not include students was made in Victoria in recent years. Students at Year 12 level were given the opportunity of particpating in the design of courses which could then be accredited by the governing educational body. In some learning centres women negotiated courses of study to suit their own aims and interests; using this subject material, they then prepared for a Year 12 accredited course. In this way, the course content was their own, yet it was legitimated in mainstream education by accreditation by a recognised educational body. Unfortunately recent changes in Year 12 requirements threaten the availability of this valuable experience. When the student participates in course design, the inherent ability to control the curriculum which is a feature of most credential systems is replaced by a degree of control by the student. At the same time, she can gain the status associated with formal assessment if that is what she desires. In this way the life experiences of the mature-age student are called upon to shape her understanding of her needs in education. By satisfying these needs, she learns about her own experiences in a wide social and historical context, and she satisfies the requirements of society and particularly the workplace for a recognised credential.

There seems to be a great difference in teacher attitudes to mature-age students. Those who teach in classes specifically for women have very often been through their education at a later age, or have chosen to teach in this environment because they empathise with these students. One woman said she felt very grateful because her teacher in a college of advanced education had not treated her like a 'dill'. On the other hand, although many women in my sample praised the patience and concern of their teachers, there were a number of complaints. The most scathing came from a woman who attended a northern suburbs high-school evening class to study for the HSC. She said,

★ I feel slightly patronised being a mature-age student among younger people. It also appears to me that whether we pass or not does not seem to matter much to night-class teachers. I get the feeling they are only there to collect their pay cheque.

When teachers are trained to teach younger students, they sometimes do not understand what older students can bring to their classes and they feel threatened. For example, a teacher of adult students who attend ordinary high-school day classes with younger students obliquely revealed his view that experience and subject matter are quite distanced from each other. In a statement which was meant to placate the teacher who felt threatened by the life experience of the older student, he said:

★ Teachers have to feel comfortable. There's no academic challenge. Although mature-age students have a greater understanding of the *world* than kids, they will not have any greater understanding of the *subject* than other kids. Once you realise that, you can relax as a teacher. (The emphases are his)

A further twist to the problem of using or ignoring adults' life experience is added in the following observation from the same source:

★ They've 'been there, done that'. The stuff on family in human development—they know it, but they don't know that they know it! One got an 'A' and the other three got 'Bs'.

A method of teaching that Michael Young presents to counter the situation where subject matter is removed from experience is referred to as 'curriculum as practice'. This focuses not on a structure of knowledge but on 'how men collectively attempt to order their world and, in the process, produce knowledge'. The method requires that teachers do not 'hand down' academic discoveries, but collaborate with pupils to accomplish knowledge. Young argues that the political and economic character of education sets limits on the possibilities of curriculum and teachers as agents of change, and concludes that 'if the educational experience of both teachers and pupils is to become a realistic possibility of human liberation, then this is going to involve . . . much action by teachers and pupils that would not be seen as either confined to schools, or in conventional terms, necessarily education at all'.

The fact that the students, as well as teachers, are adult and not necessarily confined to the formal school situation suggests that in adult education there is a possibility for learning to contribute to human liberation. Basic to the teaching method is a thorough understanding by both teacher and student of the adult's needs in terms of improved image of self, as well as an appreciation of the life experiences which both shape and inhibit individual development. An interviewee previously involved with the management committee of a women's learning centre illustrated the potential that adult education has for the production of knowledge in her comment:

★ I saw that learning and education was not just something that went on in the classroom. I knew what had happened to me. I knew how much I had learned just from doing it and wanting to do it. Other people would learn by going through the same process. People took things on and blossomed. They got so much self-esteem from finding they could do these things.

When high and technical schools offer preparatory and Year 12 classes to adults, there is often an assumption that they will teach the required body of knowledge in the same way as they teach it to school students. My study, as well as my experience with adult learners, suggests that many women have the same expectations, referring to 'born' teachers and their own 'gold star' mentality as evidence that they see their adult education as belated schooling.

A report on returning to secondary study in Victoria quoted the observations of several high-school teachers that mature-age students actually require to be 'spoonfed' and have to have work 'set' for them. One referred to this need as 'a little external regulation just to keep them on the track'. The organiser of a women's program at an institute of technology warned that informality should be gradually introduced as many of those returning to study have memories of a more formal education system and are not ready for too much informality at first. In my own experience as a teacher of the HSC at a high-school evening class, I found that the adult students, mainly women, expected to be given 'correct answers', and were at first loath to explore issues themselves, or to relate them to their own experiences, not because the environment was unduly threatening, but because it was not their expectation of adult education.

Some formal subjects for accreditation, particularly legal studies, economics, and some sections of human development and society, are difficult to relate to one's experience and constitute an area of almost rote learning that deprives it of any possibility for creative teaching methods. Other subject matter such as English, literature, history, women's studies, politics, and sections of the human development and society course can also be taught in a 'Skinnerian' fashion, where the learner has little input: content to be learned is clear and evaluation is based on measurement of expected outcomes. On the face of it, these methods are acceptable to many adult learners who see their needs fulfilled in passing examinations and gaining credentials. Alternatively, these subjects, and no doubt others (when one considers the philosophy of science and mathematics) can be presented in such a way that the knowledge is personalised.

A recent Ministerial Review of Postcompulsory Schooling in Victoria refers to such a teaching method when it is suggested that 'all individuals should take responsibility for participating in the design and implementation of social solutions'. More specifically, it is claimed that a study of work in its changing forms 'would enlarge the perspective beyond that of the individual . . . ' The emphasis is on the individual becoming part of the wider community by *understanding* its structure. The adult, with her life experience, has the potential to go further. She can, by sharing with others her experience of, say, the work situation inside or outside the home, not only understand that particular structure of society, but can *reflect* on its ideological underpinnings and how these affect her personally. This stage of critical reflection, when new experiences are assessed on the basis of our assumptions and life experiences, is uniquely an adult one, since few young students have experience of social structures outside the home and school on which to reflect.

The difference, then, between understanding a social structure, such as work, and being critically reflective of it, lies in whether the information under consideration is intellectualised or internalised—whether it is understood in abstract or concrete terms. Although a study of work enlarges the individual's perspectives and provides information on which to base plans for the future, it may not question assumptions about work. For example, it may not raise the issue of what one interviewee callled 'non-work', that is, work done in the home and the community for which no money is paid. I consider that for many women study for credentials and paid work outside the home is the means by which they overcome a widely held assumption that their contribution to society is not valid, and certainly not worthy of being accorded high status. Many early-retired and unemployed people share this view of themselves. If this assumption is not questioned in a study of work, it does not confront the type of thinking that perpetuates the sense of low self-worth that many people feel even when they enter the workplace in low-status jobs. This is not to say that the need for individuals to work is under question, but rather that the relationship between measurement of self-worth and work are analysed and understood.

With such a range of possibilities within which a provider must establish the needs, both educational and personal, of prospective students, for example, subject choices, times of classes, childcare and counselling, it is obvious that the philosophical and ideological perspective of the institution must contribute considerably to the organisation of a learning environment. In education for women, I see two fundamentally different notions of what they need. There are learning institutions that serve the student who responds to the demands of the education system, and those that attempt to serve the more profound needs of adults for control over their own learning and subsequently their own lives. The latter type sees control over their own learning as an integral part of the development of autonomous individuals. The mature-age student can go directly to the formal education system, often without understanding the forces and influences in her life which drive her. She can gain important credentials, but she may never feel free of a sense of powerlessness in her paid or unpaid place of work. In view of the numbers of women who return to study for self-improvement, need can be seen in the desire to change one's view of self; even when the adult woman has a career in mind, her education is the means by which she intends to improve her self-image and her status. It has been claimed that women who complete their degrees and assume professional responsibilities increase in confidence, self-esteem and assertiveness. But what of those who do not, or those who had no intention of 'assuming professional responsibilities'? Even those who do sometimes carry on the dual roles of work and home with little or no help because they do not feel entitled to ask for it. As I suggested in the first chapter, gaining credentials satisfies a need for achievement in our competitive society, but for many, confidence, improved self-image and assertiveness are not necessarily outcomes of their adult education.

While my research has concentrated on the adult woman, I see similar implications for unemployed people, both male and female. It would be foolish to underestimate the status associated with paid work, but it is equally foolish to overestimate the status that will come simply through gaining credentials. The view of self can best be enhanced by a clear understanding of the social assumptions and values which shape our thinking, including a critical awareness of the value of formal education. Status, that is, a measurement of worth ascribed by circumstances such as occupation, socioeconomic position and education, can then be understood as part of a hierarchical structure which underpins our society. The decision to try to move upward through that structure, or to reassess personal worth by other criteria, such as effectiveness in a small group, for example, a family or a local community, is then a considered one and one that has the potential to enhance self-esteem.

Adult education and change

If we understand that educational practice reflects educational philosophy, it can be seen that a traditional view of education basically as a means of transmitting 'knowledge' will be reflected in a formal practice. But the assumptions underlying that view of knowledge can be questioned. We might ask, 'Does this knowledge relate to the experience of the mature-age student? If not, why not?' One woman commented that her teacher education course was not designed to take into account the experience that adults bring to their study. If this question is asked by those who provide adult education, it shows a concern with the connection between education and personal and possibly social change. If they do not subscribe to the notion of 'transmitting' knowledge but rather to its being built up from a sharing of personal experiences which are interpreted in their wider social contexts, for example, of race, class, gender or religion, then the resulting educational practice will necessarily be different from formal or traditional practice.

For the purpose of comparison, I use the term 'informal' to describe educational practice that gives high priority to life experiences as a learning source. The word 'informal' could as well be 'non-traditional' in that it breaks away from a view of education that has been sustained for many years in our society. The physical environment and teacher-student relationships are generally less formal than in traditional institutions, although there are necessarily varying degrees of formality in its organisation. By the same token, there are many aspects of 'informality' in mainly traditional institutions and courses.

The criteria on which I have categorised learning situations as 'formal' or 'informal' are:

Curriculum
FORMAL: *Presented as 'fact'; a body of knowledge explored and assessed mainly for the purpose of gaining credentials*
INFORMAL: *Presented as 'practice'; emphasis on issues as starting point from which to gain knowledge about self and environment*

Physical environment
FORMAL: *School classrooms, lecture theatres, rooms in large institutions with traditional furniture*
INFORMAL: *Houses, community centres with furniture/facilities which allow an informal atmosphere*

Childcare
FORMAL: *Sometimes available, depending on demand, or on initiative of user group*
INFORMAL: *Considered as a basic requirement for participation in adult education*

Recruitment of teachers
FORMAL: *By large institutional provider*
INFORMAL: *By community group, or by funding body which generally appoints those with interest in informal learning*

Teaching methods
FORMAL: *Largely traditional methods of lecturing and teacher-led discussion and analysis*
INFORMAL: *Emphasis on using experience of adult to personalise knowledge*

Adult student involvement in curriculum development
FORMAL: *Minimal because of policy of curriculum development by the institution itself or by a state body*
INFORMAL: *Policy of trying to seek out needs by discussion with users who are encouraged to participate in decisions on curricula*

Philosophy of education for adults
FORMAL: *Usually based on traditional view of education as a relatively hierarchical structure*
INFORMAL: *Largely encompassing the 'de-schooling' values of Illich, and sometimes the philosophical approach of Freire*

As I have pointed out, there is a degree of overlap between formal and informal adult education based on these criteria, but the differences, and thus the grounds for comparison and debate, rest largely on the educational philosophy of the body which provides the facility. It is important for women students to understand these different approaches to learning. Although it is unlikely that many tertiary institutions would move far from

their traditional patterns of lecturing and tutoring, it is valuable
to understand the weaknesses and strengths of this system so
that one is not overwhelmed by it. With knowledge of learning
methods in other environments, the adult student is in a position
to expect that she will participate fully and equally with the
teacher and other students in producing her own knowledge.
This is the essence of learning and a positive means of improving
self-esteem and confidence.

Most people know about traditional places of learning for
adults, such as high-school evening classes and tertiary
institutions, but informal ones are not as well known. Learning
groups are often formed by groups of women who become
concerned about some problem or issue, or become aware of
some useful function that they could perform for themselves and
for others. For example, one women's learning centre evolved
from a church group where several women said they did not
want to join the Red Cross or attend the school mothers' club.
They felt there should be something more demanding for them
to do. Their centre began as a craft venture, but developed into
an educational focal point for the community. Another centre in
a working-class suburb was started by a woman who saw the
need of others like herself for social contact. The essential
element in adult learning environments of this kind is group
discussion, which serves the dual purpose of ameliorating social
isolation and providing a forum where ideas can be expressed,
debated and legitimised. In a sense, these groups are producing
their own knowledge. Sometimes they expand and respond to
the demands of the community for more formal education, such
as preparation for Year 12 examinations, but the method of
learning is maintained. For the woman with little sense of
personal identity the opportunity to speak and be heard in a
small, unthreatening group can be the beginning of a process of
change that is irreversible. A number of statements made during
interviews attest to the importance of the group in learning for
adult women.

★ Just talking with others at the Co-op I learnt a lot about myself and
where I fit in.

★ It make me reflect on my own life, socially and politically. You start seeing yourself in a discussion group. It draws you in.

★ I know there was something more to life than just education. Coming here and being part of this group. I have started finding a life for myself and it's wonderful.

★ At first I was scared. I underestimated my capacity to learn, talk, mix with other people in varying degrees. I feel that we all felt the same. I listened and I learned—not so much what was in books, but ideas, opinions, what was right or wrong. I learned mostly about myself. I learned that being housebound with four babies did not make me a vegetable. All it needed was the stimulus. My ideas changed—not radically, but changed nonetheless,

★ You can try ideas here that you would not think of saying outside. You're not someone's wife or mother.

★ I liked best learning in a class of women only. They are more co-operative and non-competitive. They often share the experiences of their lives, and so self-development follows for us all. When family problems occur which could jeopardise one woman's ability to complete her study, they will find how to help and organise doing so. Teacher-student relationships are easy and equal when you share with each other common life experiences. HSC and craft classes are a means of meeting and mixing with others. This enhances sharing of knowledge and gets good exam results too!

Each of these women attended a women's learning centre which either employed its own teacher or had teachers provided by a local TAFE college. In the latter situation it was observed that the teacher had asked to be sent to teach part-time in a community learning centre because she had been a mature-age student herself and felt empathy with women with a similar need.

Some women were not so fortunate. The experience of one questionnaire respondent who attended day classes at a suburban technical school was echoed in a number of similar complaints about the difficulty of finding people with whom to share their fears and achievements. She said,

★ As you will have realised, I have tried part-time study courses, but for various reasons have given them away. The main reason is because, although I have a certain amount of free time, there was time to attend classes, but the only time left for study was after the evening meal. As this means after 9 pm allowing time for cleaning up, after one year I decided I didn't have the motivation to continue in this way. Another reason is probably the fact that there was no conducive atmosphere for study. Had I found someone with whom I could study, or had my husband or children been studying, it may have helped. Some motivation is required. And then I would not have qualified for any type of employment, which I would ultimately desire, even after completing up to four years' hard labour at the HSC.

For some women whose sense of self-worth is exceptionally low, and who are attracted to informal learning centres for non-accredited learning, acceptance by the group can be the first step in a process of self-development that may not eventually include formal education.

Another important function of women's learning centres, which helps participants to understand the social, economic and political environment in which they live, is involvement in a large number of other agencies, such as committees, local schools, conferences, community childcare associations and local government community programs.

The mystique of formal education

There is a mystique attached to formal education institutions which is maintained by a hierarchical structure and a 'professional' attitude to knowledge and its measurement. The more adults are attracted into universities and colleges before they have examined the notion of knowledge and how it is produced, the less opportunity they have for exploring other avenues of learning based on their own experiences of living in a society. By not accepting responsibility for their own learning in deference to the perceived superiority of a higher educational body, the social and cultural status quo is effectively reproduced: decisions on what is to be considered valuable knowledge are left in the hands of an unchallenged hierarchy.

When the adult student has taken a course without considering that she might be leaving unchallenged assumptions upon which the course is constructed and taught, the only person who can redress the situation is the teacher, but, at the same time, the teacher is in a position to be unduly influential. For example, it has been claimed that university educators could help to produce consciousness in those who will take part in producing the next generation, thus contributing to non-reproductive education, by politicising the students. These strategies involve 'transformative pedagogies' which include developing counter-ideologies. Such an approach could, however, lead to a transference of dependency from one ideological assumption to another without inviting critical reflection by the individual.

Demystification of the education system can take place if it is examined as one of the institutions of our society which has great influence on both society's values and the way individuals measure their own worth. By relating her personal experiences to this examination, the student works towards a synthesis of experience and awareness. Issues which might have been seen as intensely personal ones are then universalised. This philosophy of education is encapsulated in a statement by the Association of Neighbourhood Learning Centres which I mentioned in the previous chapter, but which I repeat here to illustrate my point.

★ Courses are *only the means* by which people come together to share their problems, to verbalise their needs and to gain confidence in themselves as socially necessary human beings, to stimulate awareness of their rights as individuals and to develop a social consciousness as people and members of a wider community. [their emphasis]

I digress a little here because I want to point out just a few of the problems I discovered in maintaining this view of adult education.

The problems of establishing needs, delegating authority, and maintaining an adult educational philosophy are obvious even in the most autonomous of informal learning environments. A paradox arises when one considers that a philosophy which espouses the delegating of authority is at risk if no one takes responsibility for perpetuating it. The person who does take such responsibility can be regarded as autocratic, as was reported by interviewees from one women's learning centre. When discussing the philosophy of the centre with a group of ten of its ex-students, I was aware of positive and negative responses to this type of environment. There was a feeling that they were being manipulated in a way they did not really understand. This could simply have been their response to challenges to assumptions about society which they had held for some time. One of the ten felt that there was a difference between the philosophy and the reality of the establishment and was quite bitter about her experiences. Eight agreed that their lives had taken different directions since their involvement with the centre. The following excerpts give some indication of the changes in views of the world that they had experienced:

★ Any demonstration that I have made came from that atmosphere. I've written many times to the *Age* since then.

★ I wanted to learn the simply basic things. I wasn't very interested in nuclear energy or finance but then I was glad to learn about people and what was going on.

★ I was unaware that M. was making us think about things. She would say, 'This does affect you'. Was she a radical? No, she was probably finding out too. She was socially aware. She had not taught adults before so it was a learning experience for her.

In this chapter I have attempted to point out the subtle differences between education and learning as I have observed them in both formal and informal adult education environments. Encompassing the broad spectrum of education from pre-HSC and informal consciousness-raising classes to postgraduate courses, it has been necessary to make some comparisons between situations which, it may be argued, bear no comparison, for example, a Master of Arts degree at a university and 'English for Fun' at a women's learning centre. Certainly, the stated aims of each education provider are different, the one being primarily concerned with attaining a specific formal educational objective and the other with attaining objectives of personal development and understanding of self. However, as adult women who, regardless of their previous educational attainments, have shared similar experiences as wives, partners, mothers, members of the workforce and of the wider society, I contend that it is vital at all levels of return to study that they first understand these experiences in the context of the social forces and structures which direct their lives. This understanding requires that mature-age women students develop critical awareness of the society in which they live and the place of the formal education system within that society.

While formal places of learning can provide additional support systems for women, and many do, and individual teachers can try to break down the hierarchy of the formal teaching system, these methods only serve to camouflage the basic structure of the education system as one in which very few women achieve high status. If informal learning environments were to become the doors through which women chose to enter formal education, or, alternatively, through which they could choose to walk away, one of the major bastions of our male-centred society, the traditional education system, would be challenged. Those who chose to enter formal education would do so armed with an understanding of its hierarchical and potentially conservative nature, thus being in a position to challenge such assumptions as subject choices for women. Those who chose not to pursue higher education would do so not because of any feeling of intimidation but because they had consciously rejected its values and had gained an understanding of self-worth based not mainly on the gaining of credentials, but on other criteria, such as the ability to function successfully in a group as participants in learning, decision-making and administration.

THREE
YOU FEEL CONFIDENT
AND YOU FEEL GUILTY

★ Am I different because I have a piece of paper to say I have an HSC or a Bachelor of Arts degree? Yes, because I now have hard evidence of my ability, but then again, no, because my 'other' life is virtually unaffected.

This piece of self-analysis offered during one of the interviews illustrates the type of uncertainty that I perceived in many conversations with women who had returned to study. There is a wonderful sense of freedom in pursuing something that you have always wanted to do, or in taking a new direction in your life. It is a heady experience, and in many circumstances the confidence that comes from success leads to improved communication with partners, children and friends. Yet there are often limits to the improved view of self that study brings. In fact, one woman said that although she had reached her educational goal, she felt that she had done irreparable damage to her children in the process. In this chapter I want to explore some of the influences on our thinking and some attitudes of others which help to build or undermine confidence. I contend that the negative feeling of guilt should not be able to live in the mind of a truly confident person. Of course, it is a complex problem to unravel the tangle of preconceptions and assumptions we have. There are many psychological, historical and personality-related factors which contribute to the way in which we see ourselves. I am primarily interested in the contribution that adult education makes to the self-image and status of the mature-age woman student.

First, I will discuss any changes in themselves that the women in my sample perceived, for example, improved confidence. One would think, perhaps, that such a change in self-image would necessarily lead to actions which might have an effect on the status of the adult student in the home, the workplace, or the community. Some women do make these changes, for example in expecting and receiving a sharing of household responsibilities with partners and children. Others do not. To borrow a profundity from the Bard, there is often a gulf between thought and the deed. But why? *Why* do so many women shine in the glory of achievement of academic excellence, yet continue to have a sense of low self-worth in other situations? To try to answer this question from the point of view of the contribution of adult education to self-image and confidence, I have traced, through my data, some of those niggling self-doubts which act as a brake on action, even when the self-image is improved through education. I am mainly interested in the experiences in their adult education which contribute to improved confidence or actually detract from it, but other important factors, such as attitudes of others, must also be considered. Ideally during the education process these attitudes should be discussed and weighed for their validity or otherwise. It seems a shame that many women can reach a high degree of academic success without understanding the forces in society that influence both their own and other people's views and actions.

Confidence

A very common phrase used in relation to the way women see themselves as a result of returning to study, both in the interviews and in the unsolicited comments in the questionnaires, was 'more confident', although the interviews revealed some of the parameters of the newfound confidence. For example, an arts graduate said:

★ I feel quite confident but not when I am mixing with other academics. I still see myself as lacking.

A first year arts student who gained the HSC as an adult before going to university still had difficulty speaking in tutorials because she so lacked confidence. Another third year arts student whose marks had been very high had difficulty in accepting the fact that she was determined and clever. Her self-image had changed little:

★ I may be a little bit more important in my own view, but I don't think any one else sees me as very important.

A business studies graduate, who was working as a personnel officer, was still not confident in herself and suggested that it might be the conditioning that a woman's place was to defer and be modest that is the most difficult hurdle to overcome. I noticed this deference to the authority of the teacher or lecturer in many of the conversations concerning the actual learning environment. In fact, it was often a matter of concern to the adult woman that younger students were less restrained than they were in their responses, particularly at high school. Here an assumption about the hierarchical structure of education should be questioned: that the teacher-student status difference should apply when both are adults. This is an important question and I point it out again to suggest a means by which the adult student might improve the way she feels about herself. She is not always the one who is lacking. Education which asks such questions about its own structure and those of other social institutions can go a long way to ensuring that confidence is developed in herself as well as in her abilities as a student.

For Peg, an arts student, confidence was tempered by some regret:

★ I now know there is no reason why my interpretation of an event is not as good as anyone else's. I feel confident, except that people who have known me before I became enlightened aren't prepared to accept the idea that my ideas are worth listening to. Study leaves you in a state of limbo. I feel saddened because I am not really one of them. I really admire those women who can enjoy trivialities.

Let me give you the findings from the interviews regarding this sometimes elusive, sometimes enduring confidence. Of the

46 interviewees, almost half mentioned the surge in confidence they had when teachers were encouraging or when they achieved good marks and passed examinations, although four of them placed explicit limits on their newfound confidence. Six reported a continued lack of confidence and nineteen perceived little or no change.

Of the 21 who had gained confidence, eight related this to teacher attitudes and encouragement, five to the obtaining of credentials and eight to a combination of both of these. Four gained confidence despite active discouragement from teachers. Seven of the 21 who perceived gains in self-confidence said that they had also acquired the ability to express opinions in most situations, that is, positive action had resulted from the change in self-image. Four of these students had attended women's learning centres where they commented on the administrative and organisational skills they acquired, as well as the environment where they were encouraged to talk about their own life experiences in the context of issues under discussion in the course. The remaining three had attended classes where group discussion was encouraged and contact between class members had continued outside class.

Three of the six interviewees who continued to lack confidence were encouraged by teachers, while three suffered apathy or active discouragement. Credentials, for the sake of having gained them, were important to four of them, but for the other two, who saw them as a stepping stone to a thoughtfully chosen career, they were a means to that end only. These two were high achievers in areas not traditionally frequented by women, accounting and business studies, and they claimed that the prospect of success in their lucrative and comparatively high-status careers would help to overcome their present lack of self-confidence.

In the experiences of those six interviewees who spoke of continued lack of confidence, it was difficult to isolate any one factor, but a number of similarities did appear. For example, all had been subjected to patronising attitudes and actions either by employers, teachers, or family members. One interviewee's experiences revealed some of the social attitudes and actions which have shaped women's views of self and which have an effect on their choices. Sarah, aged 34 and studying accounting, was the first graduate in her family of origin and is married to a professional man. She described her mother's occupation as 'home duties', but remembered at a very early age not wanting to be like her mother, 'not because I disliked her or perceived her to be unhappy but because I have known always that that life was not for me'. Although she could think of no positive role model in her life, she did attend a very academic school for girls in England where she developed an ambition to study law at Cambridge. On returning to Australia in 1965, she was discouraged by teachers because 'girls don't do law because they can't get jobs'. A postscript to the interview, received by mail, suggested a need for affirmation of personal identity, despite her outstanding achievements.

★ I have found this studying business very, very lonely at times. I'm caught in a limbo land—*not* a full-time mother, which *can* have social advantages, *not* a working mother, *not* a full-time student, which can also be a very social activity. So, although I may appear to be in complete control, it is pretty difficult and it requires this great faith in eventual success and employment—deferred gratification at its most distant! [her emphases]

The observations on the gaining of confidence, or otherwise, as an outcome of returning to study led me to explore the possibility of connections between gains in self-confidence, the gaining of marks and credentials, and the attitudes and actions of teachers towards adult women students. The latter was particularly relevant considering that nearly half the respondents volunteered comments about teachers.

Teachers and the building of confidence

In chapter 2 I pointed out the different types of teacher-student relationships and learning environments and their potential to foster or inhibit change in view of self. Here I want to look more closely at the means by which confidence is gained or limited. The relationship between attitudes of teachers of adult women and the development of self-confidence in their students is undoubtedly very important. Nearly a third of the respondents to the questionnaire commented on encouraging attitudes of teachers, while a few mentioned teacher apathy or discouragement.

I suggest that, in some cases, improved image of self is not sustained, or is limited, because teacher attitudes are shaped by teachers' perceptions of what the adult woman student *needs*. For example, she may assume that she needs only to be encouraged in her efforts to succeed in her chosen course, whereas her need may be much deeper. She may need to know and understand why she lacks confidence and why achievement is so important to her. This suggestion will be criticised by those who are genuinely pleased with the encouragement of their teachers and with their own academic success. I certainly do not mean to disparage those achievements and the contribution they make to one's self-image. In fact it is very difficult to continue studying if teachers' comments are too scant or not at all encouraging. I do, however, wish to alert my readers to the fact that this confidence is based on success in one field, education, and that is part of a whole socially constructed network of factors by which status is measured. No doubt a degree of self-esteem is earned by achieving according to society's decreed measurements of worth, but unless the learning environment encourages analysis of the social structure in which we live, there is a danger that the adult woman student will develop a rather precarious view of self. It may be quite adequate in some situations and dismally inadequate in others. Ideally, returning to education should provide an opportunity for women to understand not only the subject material and their courses but the influences, encouragements and contraints to which they are often unwittingly subjected.

It seems that teacher encouragement can take two forms: encouragement to sustain the rigours of exam preparation by teaching the required skills and making allowances for specific problems such as family commitments and deadlines and, second, the provision of support and therefore encouragment by facilitating group dynamics, the exchange of ideas and discussion of problems and issues. These are not mutually exclusive ways of encouraging the student. I separate them to clarify my point that the first is more limited in its potential to build confidence in the adult woman than the second. It can produce confidence in academic ability without necessarily being accompanied by sustained improvement in self-confidence. The second method can bring confidence based on an understanding of the forces at work in society and can lead to a better understanding of self in relation to those around us.

Comments from some of the sixteen interviewees who mentioned teacher attitudes as contributing to their confidence reveal that the type of encouragement does differ significantly. The comments of five women show confidence gained from a teacher's encouragement by giving good marks and showing interest in the student's progress.

★ I nearly gave up once or twice but the teacher was very encouraging. She gave me good marks. (Rosemary, HSC at a Council of Adult Education class)

★ B. inspired me with confidence. She suggested I should go on to university. (Deirdre, HSC, at a women's learning centre, now at university)

★ This school is small; teachers like Mr C. are interested and very encouraging and he asks me about my marks. The girl in the library is very helpful, but I have no close friends in class. (Dora, Year 11 maths and English at a high-school evening class)

★ After a couple of weeks I realised I had it [intelligence]. I had two very encouraging male teachers who gave me good marks. (Laura, HSC at a high-school evening class, now at university)

★ In the first year I had two tutors who were very sympathetic to the fears of mature-age students and my study skills and essay-writing soon improved. (Claire, arts degree at university)

Five other comments show confidence gained through group discussion facilitated by the teacher.

★ The teacher was very important. She was quiet, gentle and

encouraging and we formed a sort of group where we could discuss most things. It wasn't the same in the second year but it didn't matter by then. (Joan, HSC at a high-school evening class)

Joan summed up the change in self by the comment, 'I'll never be as meek again'.

★ At the Co-op [women's learning centre], you are never put down. It inspired confidence to read and to question what might never have occurred to you. (Julie, HSC at women's learning centre, now BA at an institute of technology)

★ The teacher is very busy. She comes in for classes and has to leave immediately but she is very encouraging. We share our essays in class and I have become very confident about my ideas. It's better at the learning centre though because people have more time and there is a place to have coffee and talk. (Dianne, HSC at a Council of Adult Education class and also Women and Further Education program at a women's learning centre)

★ At the House [women's learning centre], we learnt from other people. The teacher kept us on the track. Education is not separate from our own experience. I went to the high school to do politics because I thought they were not getting enough done at the House, but I realised I was really learning. (Moira, HSC at a women's learning centre and a high-school evening class, now at university)

★ Lessons at the evening classes were quite informal. The teacher created an atmosphere where we could discuss. If I had started where I am now, I don't think I would have stuck at it. (Jenny, HSC previously at a high-school evening class and later at a high-school day class)

The teacher Jenny referred to had felt obliged to take the adult class when no one else wanted it because she had been a mature-age student herself. Comments on the questionnaires and those made during the interviews also suggest that some teachers do not see the teaching of adults as very important, and some are blatantly patronising. Nell, a 45-year-old student of the HSC, said that she could hear the unspoken 'old' in the voice of her male teacher at a suburban high-school evening school when he asked the question, 'And what does Nell think of this?' She knew of others who had dropped out of classes because the teachers were not interested in the views of adults.

Although many teachers were encouraging in the academic areas, they sometimes did not realise the pressures on adult students with family responsibilities. Colleges and universities appeared to provide less support by way of teacher availability and encouragement than did secondary and informal venues. For example, a third year arts student encountered two conservative academics 'who slighly resented mature-age women students as being hardly worth educating'. Another suggested that they were encouraging within their own disciplines, but were not interested outside their own departments. Some of them made no special considerations for problems connected with children's illnesses or other family matters. This is not to say that mature-age women are not welcomed into academic studies. A report on these students in higher education in Australia found that tertiary lecturers and tutors generally were pleased to have mature-age students in their classes, although a small number of younger staff members felt threatened. I simply point out that encouragement in the chosen course of study generally contributes to an increase in confidence, but both student and teacher should understand that this is only one aspect of the woman student's life and one about which she often feels ambivalent. Should I be here when my child is sick? Should I have taken this on when I have so many other demands on my time—children to collect, shopping . . . ? Do I have the right to be here?

While not mutually exclusive, it seems that the formal learning institution employs teachers whose emphasis lies in encouragement for further academic achievement, while the informal environment places more importance on the teacher as facilitator of group participation and discussion to develop communicative skills, and hence confidence in one's opinions and values. It is significant that four of the seven interviewees who claimed that their increased self-confidence had led to the ability to express opinions in most situations had begun their adult education in a women's learning centre. The other three had experienced learning in an environment where the teacher had the ability to draw out the opinions and life experiences of the mature-age students in an effective group situation. When there is an opportunity for fears and uncertainties to be aired in a supportive situation and this is considered a valuable part of the learning process, the person's confidence grows with her understanding that she makes a valuable contribution to a complex social system. Academic achievement has a place within the system but improved confidence based on this factor alone is limited.

You have to learn the language

In the course of the interviews, many students commented about the type of language they had encountered. For some, the language used by lecturers and teachers hindered the development of their own confidence because they felt personally lacking in understanding. One interviewee admitted having taken her tape-recorder into the first year English lectures at tertiary level so that she could then listen to them at home and interpret them with the aid of a dictionary. Students of sociology spoke of having to learn the 'jargon'. Others found the assumptions of teachers about their knowledge of essay-writing and language skills quite difficult to cope with. Even when not directly asked for information in this area, some of the questionnaire respondents mentioned difficulty either with the language used by the teacher or with their own language skills. The following extracts from interviews supply evidence of some of the problems associated with language and its effect on the way they see their own abilities.

★ I find difficulty in putting thoughts into acceptable terms, for example, 'juxtaposition'. I listen to the beauty of words, hear terms, but never get to use them. The head of the English Department speaks beautifully, but he leaves me wondering what he is talking about. (Janet, BA at university)

★ In fine arts and English, it is very 'clicky'. You have to pronounce French words correctly. The tutor intimidated me by his use of language, but he was a good tutor. (Rhonda, BA at university)

★ I sat in the first lecture for three hours and did not understand one word. It could have been Chinese. A friend said, 'You'll learn the lingo'. (June, graduate diploma in health education at a college of advanced education)

★ You become 'academic wise'. You learn what all the terms mean but you don't always get to use them yourself. (Lena, BA at the institute of technology)

Annette, a BSc student, had a more pragmatic view of the learning situation.

★ Every new subject has its jargon, but lecturers usually explain the terms. The lecturers are not social. They deliver high-powered stuff, and can't get away from it.

The linguistic skills of leaders in the business or political world can be compared with those of a teacher or lecturer. The person or student, man or woman, who is unfamiliar with the language is overwhelmed by it, perceiving himself or herself to be lesser in some way. One has only to consider the numbers of women in relation to men in politics, the government bureaucracy, at the top levels of business enterprises and secondary and tertiary educational institutions to argue that comparatively few women have access to the language that will allow them to see themselves, and to prepare to be, in positions of power. They may choose not to seek these positions, but unless they are aware of the possibility that language can sustain a feeling of powerfulness or inadequacy, they will still feel overwhelmed by its use in academic, business or social situations.

Confidence and self-esteem are obviously very closely related. I have also come to understand that these two concepts are affected by how one perceives one's place in the power structure of society. Let me explain. If I feel that I am 'just a housewife', or 'just a clerk-typist', or a student who is overwhelmed by the language used by my teachers, I am positioning myself at a distance from what I see as the important, or powerful, positions in society. In that sense, I see myself as dominated by a more powerful person or a group. In the family, the 'just a Mum' person allows herself to be placed in a relatively low position in the family power structure. The feelings of guilt when attempting to find an identity elsewhere—which I shall discuss later in this chapter—attest to that. In the learning situation, the student often replicates this power position because she sees the mastery of language skills as a measure of the superiority of her teachers. In other words, language becomes an effective means of maintaining a distance between the learned and the learner.

Undoubtedly, socioeconomic position exacerbates the problem of powerlessness. If the basic needs for food, clothing and shelter for herself and her family can be satisfied only if she works full-time, a woman will be less able than more affluent ones to become acquainted with the language of power. It is, however, my contention that many women from all walks of life do not understand the use of language as a means of maintaining a social hierarchy, and the learning situation in which many of them find themselves as mature-age students often helps to maintain their helplessness in the face of a kind of intimidation.

The authors of a French study were bitingly critical of university lecturers who never say, 'They do not understand us and it is our fault'. While admitting the difference in degrees of expertise and knowledge between teachers and students, they thought that teachers should make an effort to continually define their terms in an attempt to break down the power relationship between themselves, who appear to the student to have an inherent gift of language, and the student, who sees herself as inadequate or excluded from such discourse.

An Australian study supports the claim that languages can be a vehicle for expressing power relationships, and goes one step further in claiming that 'language is about growth of personal and political autonomy and the boundaries of social change'. I suggest that those adult students who commented on their own incompetence in either using or listening to language of expression and instruction are effectively cut off from any real sense of improved confidence in self because they do not understand the ability of language to maintain positions of power. Language can act as a barrier to a changing view of self if it is not understood that it is being used as a tool by which the existing power structure is maintained. It is only under certain learning conditions that time and importance is given to a study of the structure of our society. In some situations, the teacher assumes a dominant attitude and uses skills with language to reinforce his or her position in that particular hierarchy, thus inhibiting the growth of self-confidence.

The importance of a demystifying of language in breaking down both class and gender hierarchies becomes apparent particularly when one realises that the adult student is very often a teacher in her own home. It has been argued that 'the words we use daily reflect our cultural understandings and at the same time, transmit them to the next generation through an agency that subserves the culture's needs'. If within the family situation the mother, even as an adult student, feels in awe of those who teach her, she will perpetuate the lack of cultural understanding that makes her feel that way. In other words, without reflection on language as an agent by which power is distributed in our society, she will not overcome its symbolic violence, even if she painstakingly learns the meanings of words.

Although not directly concerned with language, the following comments seem to fit here in the discussion about the position of the adult woman student in the learning situation, and the degree of confidence she feels. They reflect some of the discomfort that many of us feel, but rarely express:

★ I started by having to learn everything. I had never heard of a tutorial. I didn't know anything about anything. We had coffee with some of the lecturers, but I had to force myself to call them by their first names. (Lena, BA at an institute of technology)

★ I felt the authority of the head of department. She was accepted in a man's world. I felt ignorant. If you failed it didn't matter because they had your money. (Lorraine, fine arts degree at a college of advanced education)

★ I was so pleased to have the opportunity to be learning what and when I wanted that I didn't want to challenge anything. Students need teacher's skills and direction—like a father figure. (Marie, fine arts degree at a college of advanced education)

It is evident from comments such as these and those directly concerning language that some adult students are aware of the social distance between them and their teachers, but they are not always aware of the implications for their own self-image.

The piece of paper: credentials and confidence

Many of the women who gained in confidence attributed their improved self-image wholly or in part to gaining credentials, even when they had no definite career prospects. Such faith in certification as a measurement of self-worth reflects the importance society gives educational credentials in assessing status, and is borne out by the following comments made in interviews:

★ Being English and lower middle class, there was no hope of getting 'up there' in England, but when I came here I realised I could do it by becoming well educated. (Lorna, BA at university)

★ You could do Council of Adult Education classes until you're 80 but never end up with anything. Go and do something that will give you credit. There is no point in studying for nothing. (advice given to a mature-age student by her sister)

Many of the mature-age students in my study not only recognised and accorded social value to credentials, but they were extremely conscientious and high achievers. There was a similar finding in a study which considered the age factor in predicting academic success. It was claimed that the better performance of older students could be explained in part by a willingness to make personal sacrifices. The notion of sacrifice was confirmed in my research, but the following interviewee was obviously sceptical of the need for this dedication:

★ Some women sacrifice themselves as if someone expected it of them.

Even given the tendency to make personal sacrifices for the sake of their interest in study, some women are reluctant to believe that their hard work actually earns success. I had many letters in this vein in response to a newspaper article I wrote in 1982. The following is an excerpt from one of those letters written by a mother of four who had reached second year at a tertiary institution:

★ I work hard and get good marks, but I am convinced that the teacher is just being 'nice' and encouraging.

I think that a low expectancy of one's abilities underlies both the need to 'sacrifice' and to be very conscientious. Any improvement in self-confidence must be measured against these factors, because it is possible that the tendencies to sacrifice oneself and to be extremely conscientious accord more with the self-image of the martyr than with that of the confident, aware individual. If the 'gold star and ticks' mentality which one of the interviewees claimed to have is analysed, it has an element of proving oneself, rather than of developing analytical and interpretative skills which would lead to an understanding of one's circumstances, including the constraints such as limits placed on personal time, money and energy which can legitimately be used outside the home, which affect one's view of self. Understanding, in turn, would lead to an informed choice. Whether the mature-age student chooses to work hard for good marks and acquire certain credentials is then a matter for her to decide. She may need them for a chosen career path or she might simply want learning for its own sake. The point is that she will not be swept along into formal education without a clear understanding of her motives and her expectations. She will realise that a sense of self-worth should be based on an understanding of one's contribution to society. An educational credential may or may not be a necessary part of that contribution. My concern is for the women who assume that attaining a certain level of education will ipso facto assure them of improved confidence in all aspects of their lives.

A 46-year-old mother of five children who was studying English literature for pleasure made an observation about the subtle pressures to which many women respond:

★ Many women tend to allow themselves to be influenced into studying either more than they are willing to do in an area that does not really interest them, simply because 'everyone else' does this/that course, and in this way they deny themselves the joy of learning what they want on their own terms.

I do not mean to decry the efforts of those, like myself, who work hard to gain credentials. I only want you to consider your underlying reason for studying, and to think about the *extent* of the newfound confidence which credentials give you. Has the power relationship at home changed? Do you still feel guilty because you are using time for yourself? Do you feel more confident at work? I know many women who are well qualified and employed in responsible jobs but still feel the same sense of guilt which comes from assumptions about 'their proper place'. I shall explore these areas soon.

Meanwhile, I want to consider something that arose in my examination of the relationship between credentials and confidence, and that is the fact that so many women said that they had had no plans or perceptions of where their study would lead when they began. I wondered whether improved self-confidence resulting from studying for credentials brought with it a reassessment of perceived life chances, or whether mature-age students simply continued to pursue the next level of achievement in the search for that elusive quality, confidence. I think it very much depends on whether the learning is personalised or whether it remains 'out there' as something to be mastered. The sense of achievement thus gained is wonderfully satisfying, but I question whether it has provided the confidence which it has the potential to develop.

Using the 'dominant' and 'dominated' dichotomy, for clarity of comparison rather than to provoke argument, I suggest that those members of the dominant group, mainly men in middle to high socioeconomic positions, have a view of the future which allows them to make long-term plans, while a system of constraints encloses the dominated, mainly women and some men in lower socioeconomic positions, in a present from which they cannot take their distance. They are compelled to make short-term plans and one-way choices. This ideal has been explained as 'open or closed temporal horizons' which affect the individual's view of self and her future possibilities. From my data, I have drawn evidence of what I see as an ad hoc progression through the educational system, which I suggest is the response of mature-age women to the constraints and assumptions about their abilities and responsibilities which they unwittingly accept. Consider two possibilities: that we adult students are so convinced that education will provide the panacea for our problems of identity and self-worth that we continue without reflection on our underlying reasons for so doing, or that we have a sense of so little control over our own futures that we are prepared to let circumstances dictate our paths. An examination of this idea might throw some more light on the limits to confidence which many mature-age women students experience.

Of course, this particular observation excludes those women who had set themselves goals for obtaining credentials, whether for vocational reasons or otherwise. Fewer than half of the women in my sample were studying in order to re-enter the workforce. The ad hoc manner in which a number of the interviewees saw their progression through education supports the notion that culturally imposed restrictions are unconsciously absorbed by many women. For example, Julie, aged 50, was studying for an arts degree. She commented:

★ It's just grown like topsy. Four years ago I had no idea I would be where I am now.

This could be seen as the result of an optimistic outlook, with each year bringing its own development. On the other hand, Julie's family commitments prevented her from making forward plans, a situation which caused some resentment. Sally, aged 36 and studying for an honours arts degree, saw her education 'like a fan opening up'. She thought, 'If others can go to college or university, why can't I?'

Three interviewees at present at university spoke of a 'natural progression' from the HSC to university. Another spoke of 'trying the water' by doing HSC English. If she passed, she would feel confident to continue; if not, she would have lost nothing. I contend that the first step should not be testing oneself against educational standards. Confidence and self-image are too precious to take the risk of failure. There are very many women who drop out after the first step either because they have failed or because resistance from family and friends was too great. In chapter 2 when discussing counselling I explained at some length the need for group discussion in a supportive environment as a first step in returning to study.

On the subject of setting and achieving goals, it has been argued that the middle class possess the ability to adopt appropriate measures to implement the attainment of distant ends by a purposeful 'means-end chain'. Here we come up against the problem of viewing women as part of a class when, in fact, their experiences as women often cut across such divisions as class and race. The interviewees in this sample were predominantly middle-class (86.5 per cent measured by traditional methods of place of living and husband's or own occupation—see Table 6 in the Appendix), but fewer than half of them were studying with definite career aspirations in mind. This has three possible interpretations. First, the theory about middle-class attainment of 'distant ends' may not necessarily apply to women who are middle class in the same way as it does for men. Second, it could be that the ideology that 'adult women do not train for careers' is so thoroughly incorporated into formal adult education that women who return to study do not question it. Third, it could be that 'distant ends' as perceived by some women relate to personal development rather than career attainment. This interpretation is given some weight by the fact that a number of the women in my sample saw some aspect of self-improvement, such as more confidence or 'self-fulfilment', as the outcome of their study.

I argue that the notion that confidence grows mainly through achievement in formal education relies on an uncritical acceptance of the knowledge thus acquired, as well as the credentials it brings, as the vehicle through which this goal can be attained. If, however, self-image is to be improved from within, that is, through understanding the self, the society in which one lives and the position one occupies within that society, another element must enter the learning experience. Again, I hasten to say that I do not decry formal education. It has the potential to serve both goals; it is certainly both a means to an end and a method by which we can understand the world, both past and present. But that understanding must be *personalised,* otherwise it is remote and unconnected to the world which we ourselves experience at home, at work and in the wider community.

The learning environment and you

When a learning environment provides a forum where students are encouraged to discuss both social issues and personal experiences as interacting processes, many of the confidence depriving factors already experienced, such as disparagement by employers, or resistance by family to their newfound interest, are seen to have universal causes rather than personal ones, and the way is cleared for personal growth. In other words, the circumstances which one perceives are challenged by a new understanding and one's view of self in relation to them is also challenged. There is some danger in this situation, however. If this new understanding is not accompanied by the confidence to accept *or* reject her present situation, the student may simply transfer indentification from one reference group to another, thus avoiding the need to think for herself. A women who has seen herself primarily in the family group could transfer her allegiance to a women's group, particularly if that group provided an environment where she felt worthwhile. A remark from one of the students I met a women's learning centre illustrates the point:
★ When I bring my work here I at least get a response. I get no comment from the family. I get more support from outsiders.
While groups do provide invaluable support, they should also develop the critical abilities of members. In the same way that formal education should be open to analysis of the assumptions on which it is structured, so should other learning environments. The aim of all education must be to foster clear thinking and individual decision-making. Sharing experiences helps to alleviate a sense of isolation, but pooling joys and agonies without using them in the learning experiences which consider the social, historical and cultural contexts of these feelings can be dangerous

for the development of autonomy of thought. Nasty words like manipulation and propaganda come to mind, words certainly not synonymous with ability to think for oneself.

I have discussed learning environments in terms of their meeting the educational needs of women. Now I want to point to some specific observations about the places of learning and their influences on women who attended them. In the course of the interviews, nine women revealed significant changes in the way they saw the world, attributing these changes to some aspect of their adult education. It is difficult to quantify such information, but it is possible to analyse it to discover factors relating to the educational environment which are conductive to such change.

★ My first teacher at university inspired me, and my experience at the [women's learning] centre has given me a profound sense of the possibilities for change in myself and in society, and the irritation that the world is such an unjust place. (Millie, MA student at university and teacher at a women's learning centre. She was, at the time of the interview, taking women's studies at a college of advanced education)

★ I wasn't conscious of this low status in the beginning [as a housewife], but I did sociology and psychology—an applied course and very practically oriented. The study not only gave me information, it affected me personally as far as my awareness. I reflected on my past. I saw things in a different way. I understood the reasons why I behaved the way I did, for example, in my relations with my parents and family. I am not an isolated person; others behave in the same way. The blinkers are taken away. (Lena, BA at an institute of technology)

★ Two things have happened. I've read a tremendous amount for my major project in the area of women's health and that has opened my eyes. The other is I have become aware of the group dynamics in the tutorial groups. I watch and recognise the power struggles. My first teacher alerted me to my abilities when he said, 'Don't knock your own experiences'. (June, community health diploma at a college of advanced education)

★ The nature of the course [sociology and psychology] posed lots of questions for me and I had to look at myself and I got angry with my position, my mother for not raising me differently, and being poor—

and the male lecturers for patronising me. I had been to a women's group with a friends some years ago, and could discuss literature with them, but didn't really use the same language, but then I began to understand. (Rita, BA at a college of advanced education)

★ It [study] has changed everything—what I expect of them [her family] and what they expect of me. About eighteen months ago things changed drastically because I became so enraged at some of the things I was doing for them. When I was doing women's studies, my husband and I discussed roles and he was horrified at what he had taken for granted. I can't believe how much I have changed. I started out by trying not to upset anyone, but now I have legitimated my position with theory. (Moira, BA at university, previously HSC at a women's learning centre)

★ I took up the offer at the institute but I feel selfish. Where is it leading? I may go back to help at the Co-op. I've learned such a lot now. I could do community work. (Julie, HSC at a women's learning centre, later a director at the centre)

★ My education has contributed to a lot of changes in me, particularly studying human development and society. I think the most important thing is to be yourself (this might sound selfish), but if you can't be yourself, you can't be who you want to be, you can't give to other people. (Marion, HSC at a women's learning centre)

An attempt to take up a graduate diploma in community education had been thwarted by the husband of the last interviewee, Marion. He demanded that she confine her interests to home and children. Although she had temporarily been forced to accept his terms, she understood the social forces at work, her economic dependence and the reasons why she had agreed to the alternatives for a short time. Her plans for the future suggest that she expects that she will be in control of the situation when the restraints and responsibilities of caring for three small children are eased.

Another interviewee, Margaret, who lived in a working-class environment, was introduced to a women's learning centre by a social worker. Her story is one of personal and financial deprivation, but her newfound abilities as an organiser of craft activities led her to establish a drop-in centre for women in her own suburb. She recalled that one of the facilitators at the women's learning centre had said, 'You can do anything'. She realised in talking with other women that she did not have to put up with the abuse and violence she had endured at home and she became angry. While her very lowly and inadequate view of self has changed and she has successfully represented her community group at a conference, she has a long way to go, compared with some of the middle-class respondents. She said she felt inadequate because of her very low standard of schooling and felt a great need to learn. Her newfound confidence was very fragile, because she had domestic and scholastic disadvantage to overcome, but her outlook and view of self had definitely been dramatically changed by her learning experience.

Of the eight examples cited above, five were attending, or had attended, women's learning centres. The educational element which appears in all but two of the extracts is an informal learning situation, provided either by the educational body itself or by a group outside the learning environment but concurrent with the adult woman's interest in study. The other important factor, mentioned in all but two cases, is the subject or subjects studied, in these examples, sociology, psychology, women's studies and human development and society. It seems that subjects which explore the structures and power relationships in society are most likely to be 'personalised' by the adult student. Sometimes this is a result of the teacher seeing this as a necessary part of the learning experience, but in other situations, the student makes parallels and comparisons with her own life experiences with or without the direction of the teacher.

Other interviewees mentioned changes in themselves which seem to have been the result of applying a solution to their problems of coping as women, as students and as members of the paid or unpaid workforce. For example, Peg spoke to the psychologist counsellor at the institute where she was studying for an arts degree. She came to understand that she had to assert herself more and that her interpretation of an event was as worthy as any other. But she said she used her new assertiveness at home because it had to be done, though she didn't like it. In other words, she was applying a *solution,* rather than *experiencing* the change in view of self that can lead to action to change a situation.

If the type of learning environment to which the adult woman returns offers the chance to develop skills and relataionships not directly related to gaining qualifications and re-entering the workforce, and therefore not directly aligned with competitive ideals, she may change as she develops the confidence to function effectively in such a participatory setting. For example, acting as a coordinator of craft teaching and then setting up a drop-in centre for women in her own suburb achieved a measure of improvement in Margaret's self-image. But the desire to move into the formal education structure must be the result of the development of a sense of personal autonomy, not simply the outcome of accepting the direction of the group to which she has become attached. When Margaret attempted a course of formal study, she was overwhelmed:

★ I tried the HSC but I felt out of it. I could not keep up. Even when I heard others talking about what they wanted to do in the pre-employment program, I felt scared.

Working-class women from educationally and financially deprived backgrounds face the problem of low self-image, as well as, in many cases, lack of formal study skills. Even when the educational environment is an informal one, and even when self-esteem is raised by successful activity in a group, the prevailing need to confront the problem of work and a degree of financial security must be met. This affects the adult education provider as much as the individual. If the mature-age student is to increase her ability to direct her own life, she must first understand the structural forces with which she is coping, then she must choose independently to confront or condone them. Sometimes the action necessary to confront barriers is too difficult to take. Insufficient basic education or antagonism from the family often inhibits action that possibly may have resulted from increased awareness of the situation. The gap between change in attitude and change in action is illustrated by the comment of Joan, who at 52 years and divorced, was studying the HSC at a high-school evening class. She had come from a working-class background, and worked as a seamstress. She credited her first teacher with creating an atmosphere in the classroom where she developed confidence:

★ I spent most of my life doing things that I hoped would please. Now I hope they like me, but if they don't, I don't really care. I don't care about marks now, either. I feel good. Anyway I couldn't afford to give up work and go to university.

She admitted, however, that this 'don't care' attitude was not necessarily translated into action:

★ I don't demand anything. I'm still not ready for confrontations.

Priorities and dependencies of long standing are not easily overcome even for the woman for whom financial security is not a pressing concern. For the working-class woman, there is a double burden.

There are a number of interesting theories on the subject of how people change themselves through learning, all of which stress the importance of discussion and reflection on the structures of society and the forces which influence our development. When the adult student can discuss experiences in the light of her understanding of how society works, she is in a position to make a choice. She can decide to change her position within that social structure, or she can decide to remain where she is. Of course, as I pointed out at the beginning of this chapter, there are many factors, to do with psychology, history and personality, which influence our ability to act even when the social influences upon us are understood. But by drawing attention to historical and social factors which help to shape the individual and society, education can also contribute to an understanding of psychology and personal growth.

A mature-age student who has the knowledge and the support to weigh the pros and cons of her decision can virtually eliminate the possibility that she could be transferring her allegiance from one set of beliefs to another. The social forces that hold her, such as the concepts of the woman's primary role in maintaining the household and its members, are then recognised, accepted, or rejected in due course on the basis of rational understanding. For many, a clarification of their circumstances would mean that their energies could be consciously directed either to alleviating oppressive circumstances, or to working within them without guilt. This process of change is often quite gradual, although one interviewee claimed that her whole attitude to life had changed dramatically when she realised how she had previously accepted a position in the household which earned little respect. It can take time for rational understanding to be followed by action. The main point I want to make is that education can lay the foundation for significant changes in your life. It is not simply a matter of gaining confidence because you are studying: it is important to learn about yourself and your environment so that you will be in control of whatever changes you choose to make or not make.

Guilty or not guilty?

★ Writing was a reputable and harmless occupation. The family peace was not broken by the scratching of a pen. No demand was made upon the family purse . . . The cheapness of writing paper is, of course, the reason why women have succeeded as writers before they have succeeded in the other professions.

Virginia Woolf summed up many of the sentiments I became aware of when talking to women about the way they felt about taking the step to return to study. When I was reading the responses to the questionnaires and transcribing the taped interviews, I notice that the word 'guilty' came up many, many times (half of the interviewees mentioned it), and I was prompted to pursue reasons. Of course, they are complex, but I decided that if so many adult women feel guilty about their action of returning to study, they must be labouring under pressures which they have accepted as normal, and which are possibly being exacerbated by attitudes of friends, family and the wider society. I have approached the problem of guilt from the point of view of the adult student herself, as well as taking into account outside factors which contribute to it, such as attitudes and actions of those with whom she is in close contact. First, I want to consider perception of self and guilt.

To feel guilty about your conduct, you must have a notion of what is considered by society at large to be correct and acceptable action, that is, by what criteria you expect to be judged. If you feel no guilt, there are three possible reasons: you are unaware of such social pressures, you are acting entirely within the prescription for acceptable action, or you have analysed your assumptions about yourself and your place in society and have *positively rejected* any notion of guilt. If you do feel guilt, it can be assumed that you do not see your actions as legitimate—a feeling that must surely detract from any possible improvement in self-image.

It has been argued that guilt invaded women's hearts after the intensive propaganda of Rousseau and his successors that women should be mothers with boundless devotion. Those of us who were growing up and having children in the fifties and early sixties appear to have been particularly well saturated with notions of 'maternal deprivation' and 'good mothering'. Women's magazines reported the finding of researchers in the field of child development and television took up the crusade by building images of a 'proper Mum'. The dual requirements of the mother's social and economic dependence as well as her necessary passivity in the domestic sphere placed women firmly in an exclusively nurturing role, any deviation from which implied irresponsibility and selfishness, and hence, feelings of guilt.

An idyllic domestic scene was painted by John Bowlby and taken up wholeheartedly by the consumer goods advertisers of the period:

★ . . . fathers have their uses even in infancy. Not only do they provide for their wives to enable them to devote themselves unrestrictedly to the care of the infant and toddler, but, by providing love and companionship, they support the mother emotionally and help her maintain that harmonious contented mood in the atmosphere of which her infant thrives.

Many writers have supported such views, modified them, and refuted them, but academic research and debate of a more critical kind, generated by maternal deprivation theory over the last 30 years, has not generally reached the popular press. Instead, the media is still largely presenting the 'proper Mum' image to which two of the interviewees specifically referred in discussing their feelings of guilt:

★ I feel guilty about the kids. I should be a 'proper Mum', you know, a full-time Mum. (Beatrice, 35, divorced)

★ I feel guilty about school activities. I don't go much now. Also, when my daughter was sick at school, I felt guilty because they had to ring her father. I am not a 'proper Mum'. (June, 39, married)

In economic terms, media emphasis on the woman's primary role in the home can be seen as boosting manufacturing and sales of domestic consumer goods. In political and cultural terms, it can be seen as a means by which women can be kept out of a crowded workplace in times of high unemployment, or given a position of lower status than men when jobs are plentiful. For some women, this supportive and complementary role is their choice, but for many it is one that leaves them at least vaguely restless or, at worst, downright miserable. Once they act to alleviate the situation there is inevitably a conflict between their own interests and their family responsibilities.

'I no longer feel guilty reading during the day'

When a woman takes time out of her day for study, whether she is employed in the paid workforce or in unpaid work at home, the ordering of her priorities of time use must change. She either has less sleep, less leisure or more help with the household tasks. Her attitude to such a change in ordering her own time is an important gauge of whether she sees her role as student as a legitimate one, and therefore one which will improve both her view of her own worth and her standing within the family. When changes in time use produce feelings of guilt, I argue that the mature-age student has undergone *no* lasting change in view of herself in relation to others, particularly the family, even though her study may have had other results, such as admiration of her determination and achievements.

Using the unsolicited comments on the questionnaires as a guide to introducing topics in the interviews, I explored changes in time use and the women's attitudes to such changes in an attempt to assess the degree of change in view of roles and responsibilities, and thus guilt or otherwise, which had occurred since returning to study. Responses to the questionnaire indicated that for just under half of the women, 'family commitments' was the reason for their undertaking part-time study, while a few combined family commitments, part-time work and study. These results indicate that, for most women, caring for the family is their primary responsibility. When the question of time use was broached, however, I was careful not to imply any judgement. For example, the question 'Do you spend more or less time with the children?' in many cases would have been a threatening question on a subject very close to the heart of the mature-age student.

In a long letter attached to the questionnaire, a 49-year-old HSC evening-class student told me that she no longer felt guilty sitting down in the middle of the day to do an essay or to read. Another 45-year-old who had completed an honours arts degree said that one of her main problems was ensuring that no one missed out on anything at home as a result of her studying. Both of these responses are the result of attitudes to the woman's role. For the first student, study was now seen to be a legitimate use of time, thus eliminating the guilt of placing her own interests first, but for the second student, her university work had to be secondary to her main function of serving the family's needs.

The needs of the family come first, or else!

Consider the following statements as evidence of the tension between the woman's interest in study and her feelings of responsibility to the family. It is tempting to ask, What would you do in a similar situation?

★ It is hard to return to study when you have a small child. There is never enough time to study . . . I am torn between furthering my own career and staying home and caring for our child and any future children we may have. There seems to be no easy answer. (28-year-old, studying for HSC)

★ As soon as I'm about to go into study time, that is the precise moment my family needs my attention. Of course, I go to them first. (33-year-old, studying for the HSC)

★ It is very difficult at times to be single-minded regarding study when faced with family responsibilities. (38-year-old, studying for BSc)

★ I felt that my devotion to my children suffered and consequently much repair work now needs to be done. The attention I should have given to my children is practically irreplaceable, and their schoolwork suffered. (38-year-old, studying for BEd)

★ I have to stress that their [the family's] needs and concerns have always come first—except when writing an essay to be handed in next day, and even then, meals are cooked, dishes washed and clothes washed and ironed as usual. (45-year-old, studying for BA honours)

Ambivalence was evident in the comment of a 42-year-old arts student who noted among the 'pluses' that she was able to help her children with their work, and among the 'minuses' that there was basic conflict of priorities between home, friends and study.

The expectation that women should always put the needs of their family ahead of their own is deeply internalised. Age, and therefore relative influence of schooling and long-held social values, the increase of women in the workforce and the women's movement do not seem to affect this expectation very much.

It has been argued that the dominant ideology in any society is perpetuated by constraining social forces, such as beliefs about the roles of men and women in society as well as by economic constraints. The occupational activity of women is experienced as much, if not more, as a moral reality than an economic one, and the notion of sacrifice is associated with it. If the mother works, the children are 'sacrificed', and if she does not, the mother is seen to 'sacrifice' her potential in the workforce for the children. Both the experience of this 'moral reality' and the internalisation of the idea of sacrifice are evident in the following comments made during a discussion at a women's learning centre:

★ I didn't want them [the family] to feel that they were being put out because I was doing something for myself.

★ We always have to check with the family that it's all right it we want to do something. We feel guilty. The husband will say, 'That's what I'm going to do', whereas the wife will say, 'Do you mind?'

★ I felt I was a self-sacrificing martyr, but the children saw me as a whinger. Now I have my study.

There is ample evidence that those who study, like mothers who work, suffer pangs of guilt about their conduct. Because I think that many of my readers will find something of themselves in the following comments, I shall include a number of the specific references to guilt made during the interviews. Admitting the feeling of guilt, sharing it and then analysing its sources is a very effective method of dealing with this negative emotion. After all, how can one's self-esteem rise when it is constantly undermined by the doubt that one is in some way misbehaving?

★ If the family is 'down', you have to be very committed to withstand the guilt. (Belinda, 40, married with two children)

★ At first I felt guilty about everyone—my mother, my children. I used to try to not let it [study] affect anyone. I prepared all the meals before going to classes. (Moira, 37, married with two children)

★ I felt so guilty I would offer to make them new clothes if they would let me study. (Heather, 41, married with three children)

★ I felt guilty at first. I was a terribly responsible wife and mother. The marriage broke up when I stopped feeling guilty. (Rose, 32, divorced with two children)

★ At first I felt guilty about dragging my child to the Co-op for meetings. (Millie, 36, married with one child)

★ I feel guilty. I ask myself if I am spending enough time with my child. (Wanda, 40, single with one child)

★ I study after the children go to bed. I feel guilty if I don't read to them first. (Pat, 32 married, with two children)

★ I feel guilty about withdrawing away from the kids. (Lorna, 37, divorced with three children)

Three of the women I interviewed felt guilty because they were studying for themselves, and not for the good of anyone else, and therefore saw this act as selfish. An illustration of the extent of acceptance of mothering as woman's primary and lifelong role can be seen from another woman's comment that she felt selfish having chosen not to have children because she knew she was not doing what her mother expected her to do.

The ideology which governs this type of thinking, that is, one that engenders feelings of guilt and selfishness, is perpetrating a type of violence on women. Granted it is symbolic rather than actual (although I have evidence of this also), nevertheless the belief that positions mothers firmly at the heart of the family and allows for the satisfaction of no personal needs acts as a brake on any transformation in view of self. It also explains how many adult women students perceive an improvement in confidence through studying, but which does not extend to situations other than the educational one. This is not to say that the legitimate demands of children should be ignored in favour of one's own needs. It is the assumption that women are naturally given to sacrifice themselves for the sake of children which should be examined. If a woman understands the social pressures that are making her feel guilty, she is more able to handle her self-doubt. She then has a choice: to conform to the traditional pattern, that is, to take primary responsibility for children and continue her study as it will fit into that arrangement, or to confront her partner, children, other family and friends with her dilemma for the purpose of enlisting their help and understanding of her needs.

The dominant ideology decrees that for economic and cultural expediency, women will defer to patriarchal authority in the home and in the workplace. By patriarchal authority I mean the type which is so structured that men are in the positions of power, either in the home as members of the paid workforce who provide the main source of money, or in the workplace itself in the most senior positions of responsibility. In the home, the authority can be maintained even by children whose demands echo the expectations of the patriarchal family that mother will be ever available.

Adult education, says Sarah, provides a resting place,

★ a halfway house where you can please everybody — and it doesn't cost much; it's not threatening. You're not earning money and maybe you will not make it.

I referred to Sarah's comment earlier when discussing motivation, but do so again because it so perfectly illustrates the conflict, as well as the compromise, that many women accept without question when they undertake a course of study. Returning to study may be the means to an end, that is, work and economic independence, or it may be a means by which women can escape domestic dissatisfaction, but for many, its potential for liberating the individual is seriously hampered by social pressures which create guilt and undermine confidence. In addition, those who provide adult education generally do not broach the subject. Social structures and their relationship with, and effect on, the individual are vital content and process areas for adult education.

A Melbourne study reveals that women returning to work suffer guilt about their children. In the sense that study is a halfway house, that is, it is *not* going to work, it could be expected that some women would not feel guilty, or would have assuaged it. However, despite evidence of a very strong commitment to family in terms of time (three-quarters of the sample were part-time students and over half claimed 'family commitments' as the primary reason for this choice), the demon Guilt still reigns supreme.

Mother? Wife? Student?—role conflict and guilt

★ When writing essays I have to ask for quiet but there are constant interruptions—time to get dinner, someone comes home, need to collect children from the train. My time is committed to others even if ideas are flowing. There is no room to study alone. (Deirdre, 47, with three children at home)

In response to the open-ended question on the questionnaire asking for any further comments on their experience as adult students, several mentioned that they experienced a conflict of roles, that is, having two separate areas of interest had become a problem to them. For others, the conflict was not recognised as such, as it surfaced only in comments on attitudes of husbands and family, to which I shall return later. When I followed up the suggestion of role conflict in the interviews, six women spoke of the debilitating effect this tension had on them, sapping energy and affecting the quality of the work produced as students and making them uncertain of the quality of their mothering.

Remaining at least technically at home, that is, not going out to work, may allay feelings of guilt for some. Many women however, let roles determine their actions, rather than acting to restructure roles for themselves, so that returning to study, but still remaining primarily in the home as the main organiser and domestic worker, can be seen as a means of assuaging any feeling of guilt associated with taking an action to improve one's self-image. After all, that 'proper Mum' or 'angel in the house' image dies hard. She is still, to all intents and purposes, behaving in a manner which does not upset the routine of the household, but at the same time she is indulging in a double life which gives her a great deal of satisfaction.

Resentment is a more aggressive sentiment than guilt, but nonetheless negative as a possible improver of self-image. Ann was married and had had seven children, three of whom were living at home, when at the age of 52 she began studying for the HSC. She said defiantly.

★ I'm going to do this in spite of them [the family] but I feel that they could give me more help.

Conflict and confusion over her perception of the extent of her family responsibilities revealed themselves in her attempts to come to terms with changes she perceived in herself.

★ Before, I let things run over me, accepted things, but now I may have been affected too much by study. I find myself fighting, but getting nowhere, but fighting. What I've tried to work out are my reactions to other people. They haven't changed. I have, but I am not going to destroy the family.

Many comments on the questionnaires spoke of 'balancing time' between study, family and sometimes paid work. Lena, aged

44, with three children, said she should have changed her attitude to household chores, but she had not. Instead, study and home (meals, looking after the family, driving them about) were 'dovetailed'. Pamela, aged 39, with three children, saw this ability to manage time as a characteristic peculiar to mothers:

★ The level of tension in the house in incredible; you're doing things but you are thinking of something else. Men don't seem to be able to do four things at once, whereas, if mothers did one thing at a time, they'd never get anything done. You do have to switch on and off.

The weighing up of advantages and disadvantages of returning to study by a 47-year-old mother of seven children illustrates both the conflict felt and the balance achieved:

★ Advantages—escape from demands and problems of family life. Disadvantages—time must be stolen from family and marriage demands and children get less attention.

The terminology is interesting. 'Escape' and 'stealing' are not the words of a woman who feels she has control over her time. They suggest confinement of some kind, again reinforcing the internalised notion that family commitments constitute a form of imprisonment—not always to be railed against, but certainly to be reckoned with when another important and interesting commitment comes into your life. Whether this reckoning induces guilt, conflict, resentment or a re-evaluation of the relationship between the woman and her family, it most certainly has an effect upon the view of self that the adult woman student holds.

Resolution of feelings of conflict and guilt

Perhaps the most obvious method of resolving these negative feelings would be to reject outright the notion of prime responsibility for the well-being and organisation of the family. It is interesting that only three of the 46 interviewees announced their freedom from guilt. Although such an important announcement could be seen as a defensive act springing from a deep-seated guilt, each women provided a degree of analysis and insight in her statement that favours the interpretation that she had genuinely overcome the social pressures that produce such guilt feelings.

Vera, aged 55, with five children (three at home), said with some satisfaction:

★ I do not feel guilty or selfish. I have looked after them for years. I got a lot out of the assertiveness program at the centre.

At first feeling guilty, Moira, aged 37, with three children, explained her development thus:

★ When I started I was determind not to change anything. We talked through problems and issues at the House [women's learning centre]. Guilt is something to do with understanding *what* is putting the guilt on you. Once you see that, you stop feeling guilty. [her emphasis]

Moira had completely renegotiated her marriage arrangements. For example, she no longer assumed responsibility for buying household goods, took holidays and outings on her own as well as with the family, and insisted that she, her husband and the children should share the household chores. Rose, aged 32, divorced and with two children, also felt guilty at first, but her involvement with a women's learning centre and the discussion that took place there freed her from guilt about her own need for education and development of self.

It has been suggested that women take arts courses as a means of avoiding conflict aroused by different expectations of career role and traditional female roles. This argument does not address the guilt which is still felt over use of time to study, but it is an interesting one in terms of conflict that might arise if the mature-age student had career aspirations which would interfere with her home role. Since over half of my research sample did not see employment as the outcome of their study, and the majority were studying humanities subjects at either secondary or tertiary level in expectation of achieving an arts degree, there is some evidence that these women see study as a means of avoiding the conflict that might arise if they chose to pursue a career. On the other hand, as I have argued in chapter 1, education is highly valued in our society as a measure of status. It can be very difficult for a woman who has left school at an early age to satisfy her need for recognition of her worth without bringing herself up at least to the educational standard of her children.

A comment by a mature-age student in a New South Wales study that she saw her time 'to be more valuable' because she was studying suggests that the uses to which women put their time is an indicator of both social expectations and evaluations of their roles. Presumably, time spent in the home is not as valuable as time spent studying. Perhaps an explanation lies in the very nature of our competitive society. The results of studying can be *measured* and thus appear to the undervalued and unpaid woman at home as a more fruitful use of time. This is not to say, however, that others see time spent in studying as valuable. A discussion I had with a group of women at a women's learning centre revealed that some husbands consider going out to work to be a more acceptable use of a women's time than studying.

Of the 45 questionnaire respondents who volunteered additional information concerning conflict or guilt, five had alleviated any sense of conflict, that is, tension between doing something for themselves and devoting themselves to their children, by recognising that their studying was beneficial to their children. Three women saw their families as a handicap to achieving their own goals and another three had made a conscious decision to put their families first, relegating their own interest to a secondary position until their children grew up.

Other conflicts

For a 50-year-old student of primary teaching, her unusually heavy family commitments were a source of embarrassment in her learning situation. She concealed the fact that she had twelve children because she did not want to be seen as 'the one with the tribe of kids'. Another 52-year-old BA student denied that a return to study contributes to a sense of personal identity. She stated:

★ Whereas I had a definite role in society before I commenced my studies, I find this is no longer so. Former friends are still involved in the organisation of fetes, street stalls, etc. for charitable institutions but in view of my full-time work and part-time study, I cannot be part of their activities. On the other hand, because of work and family commitments, I am not really a part of the student population.

She did concede that her involvement in study was the thing that had allowed her to more easily 'let go' of her children as they had grown up. In other words, returning to study had led to less reliance on the role of mother as a source of personal identity.

Previous social and parental expectations for girls has considerable effect on the way in which the present woman student sees both her domestic obligations and her personal educational needs. Girls were not expected to go very far in their education because they would 'only get married', or because only those contemplating university education needed to complete Year 12. Nearly a quarter of the sample gave their reason for leaving school as 'the normal thing to do'. Six of the interviewees spoke of their fathers' (and sometimes, their mothers') beliefs that there was no point in educating girls. Age did not appear to be a factor in the holding of this attitude, nor indeed, gender, as the following comments indicate:

★ I hated leaving school but education for girls was considered a waste of time by my father.

★ Father and mother didn't see the need to further my education, although my brother was encouraged to matriculate.

★ I was the oldest daughter. Enormous encouragement and opportunity was given to my younger brother, but it was not deemed necessary to spend the money on higher education for my sister or myself. We did nursing.

One of the interviewees' comments pointed to an authoritarian possessiveness towards the daughter as a sexual object, which influenced the father's decision to disallow further education in the field of nursing:

★ Only bad girls leave home before they are married—in his eyes it wasn't nursing I wanted but to go and live in a hostel. (Belinda, 40)

Many of the parents displayed indifference or ambiguity towards the education of their daughter, such as:

★ You're a brilliant person, a princess. You're going to university, you're going to get married—all in one breath! (Rita, 32)

There were, however, six interviewees who spoke lovingly of the influence of their fathers, who were self-taught and very encouraging to them to learn as much as they could. Two mothers were also encouraging, suggesting that their daughters should aim to be self-sufficient in case they were not always married. These mothers had supported their families alone after their husbands had left them.

It seems that, in most cases, a return to study causes some conflict, whether it is perceived as guilt or selfishness by the student herself, or whether it is in relation to the roles which society and often adult students themselves associate with women.

How others see your return to study

Attitudes of others to the mature-age woman student are a very effective means of either reinforcing feelings of guilt or conflict, or of breaking them down. The questionnaires abounded with information, all of it unsolicited, on the attitudes of husbands, children, extended families and friends.

Family members, by their support or antagonism, make an important contribution to the mature-age student's chance of improving her view of herself. On the one hand, they can act as agents of the ideology which places women primarily in the home. (Although now perhaps a little dated, submissions to the Royal Commission on Human Relations (1977) confirmed that the mother, her husband and most other people see her as the one who is ultimately responsible for the family.) On the other, they can also support her in her effort to move away from the social forces that constrain her. Together with the type of adult education she encounters, attitudes of others are important elements in the potential for improvement, or otherwise, in self-image and status that her mature-age study will engender.

What the children think

Although fourteen of the 46 interviewees, when asked about priorities of time use, answered somewhat defensively that they studied only when their children were at school or in bed, some of them did not entirely escape the displeasure of their offspring. Pamela, a science undergraduate, had a child with a maths problem which the child ascribed to her mother's involvement at university. A similar manipulative attitude was revealed in a discussion at a women's learning centre. One mother commented that the family said she did not love them any more because she stayed away from a family outing in order to finish an essay.

When the activity of study is kept from the children on the asumption that 'they might be put out because I am doing something for myself' there is an implict acceptance on the part of the adult woman student of a type of emotional manipulation. As well as this, there can be little improvement in self-image through education if it is an activity that is carried on surreptitiously. If it is not legitimate within the family, the improved view of self gained through success in education must be limited to the environment outside the home. It does not matter whether the mature-age student gains first class honours in her degree, if she still adopts an appeasing, apologetic attitude to her family, her self-image and status within that particular social group will remain unchanged.

Perhaps the attitudes of mothers and children are different in a single-parent family. Here the woman would not have the added conflict of the 'wife' role, although she may try to take on the roles and responsibilities of both father and mother. I looked at the comments of the interviewees who were separated or divorced, or who were single mothers. Four of them had supportive children and had discussed with them the need for study as a prerequisite for a good job and thus more money for the household. Both Diana, 42, and Penelope, 51, felt their children had been relieved that they were not a responsibility to them, 'moping about' and not getting on with their lives. These children were teenagers or older, and no doubt had begun to have lives independent of their mothers. By contrast, Lorna, divorced, with three children, seemed to surrender herself completely to the mother role:

★ Study comes after everything else—even after cleaning the house. I expect and get constant interruptions from the children.

Beatrice, a divorcee of 35 with two children aged ten and eight when I interviewed her, had difficulty in getting away to an evening class (chosen because she was particularly interested in the subject), and as a result had selected subjects for a proposed arts degree which were available between 9 am and 3 pm. She felt that her children's antagonism to her studying might have been a normal reaction as the children of a friend of hers 'threw a fit' at the prospect of their mother doing an arts degree after 'putting up with her two years of study for the HSC'. As I mentioned before, two women, one of whom was Elizabeth, who at 34 was separated with two children, had been accused of 'not being a proper Mum'. Another, Beatrice, offered a new wardrobe of clothes to her daughter if she would allow her to study. A seven-year-old voiced a mixture of concern and confusion about the role of his single mother when he said:

★ I wish you went to work instead to university because then you would be able to go to bed at night instead of sitting up writing esays.

I have painted a rather negative picture first, because it was quite a shock to me to discover that so many women contributed to their own guilt feelings without question. Of course, there is another side. A number of interviewees felt that the fact that they too were studying helped them to understand what was expected of their children, and in some cases was the basis of greater rapport between the two generations. However, Rosemary, aged 41, noted that her daughter was quite apprehensive about the possibility that her mother might achieve higher results in the HSC than she did. This was, in fact, what happened, and Rosemary felt duly guilty about it.

Several comments were made about the atmosphere that the studying woman created in the house—table covered with books, essays to be finished—all of which, it was suggested, contributed to a home conducive to accepting the need for higher education. An immigrant woman, speaking during a discussion at a women's learning centre, hoped that her adult sons would be encouraged to take up their education again as a result of her efforts. In one sentence, she expressed both her hopes and her tacit acceptance of the low status she had within the family: 'They [her sons] will say, "Surely if Mum can do it, we can".'

Even positive outcomes of the woman's returning to study were sometimes couched in language that suggested to me a rationalisation, a defence, or an apology. In the next chapter, I discuss changes or otherwise in various areas of the mature-age student's life, and there is more on this subject of the children and the home. Here I am concerned with the guilt or otherwise felt by the person herself.

By and large, there was little difference between the comments of those interviewees who were married or those who were living alone on their children's reactions to their studying. It comes back to the question of attitude. When a woman feels secure and confident in her own actions, that is, when she does not feel guilty that she is breaking the ground rules, the responses of those around her are more likely to be positive. Guilt often prompts a need to defend the act of returning to study, but, at the same time, the mature-age student will often appease her family for the loss of time she spends on them— Beatrice's promised new wardrobe of clothes for her children. Of course, children are quick to pick up these vibrations, as Penelope's daughter did when performing poorly at maths.

It is my opinion that while women who return to study continue to see themselves as guilty of acting in a way even slightly unacceptable to the rest of society, and, in particular, if they need to hide their interest from their family, there is no possibility that their response to study will lead to either their own social relationships changing or their effecting any change in the social attitudes of the next generation. If higher education for women who have already commited themselves to family responsibilities is seen to be relatively unimportant in relation to those responsibilities, then this type of thinking is perpetuated in the next generation. This is not to say there are not many women who willingly accept and condone this situation. Family commitment was for many of them the main reason for choosing part-time study. I do wish to make the point, however, that when a woman actively seeks to improve her self-image and status through education, it is a pity that the results have to be tempered by a vague but pervasive sense of guilt.

An understanding spouse is a boon

I have found that attitudes which dictate the roles of women and men in society may be less acted upon when the husband or partner of the mature-age student is not threatened by her intellectual pursuits. Again, it was very noticeable that when the activity of study is associated with work which will enhance the family income, these attitudes may be less adhered to. Of course, I also realise that for many women who are working at both paid and unpaid work in order to provide for the basic needs of themselves and their families, returning to study for whatever reason would be a luxury they simply could not afford. Class, in this purely economic sense, does dictate the way of life for many women. Imagine, for example, the position of a woman doing piecework on her sewing machine at her home in Collingwood. It is likely that she would feel resentment and disillusion with her lot, but unlikely that she would have the inclination or the time to return to study as a way out. For those who are interested, there is a breakdown of the socioeconomic status of the respondents in my research sample in Table 6 in the Appendix.

The real proof of whether the husband or partner has internalised traditional attitudes to the position of women is his willingness to accept the use of time for study as legitimate. Actual physical changes in responsibilities are explored in chapter

4. Here I will comment only on changes in attitude. I have found that the initiative to challenge such attitudes generally comes from the woman, and that certain elements in her educational experience will generate and sustain her confidence to make this challenge.

Much often-heated comment related to attitudes of family members resulted from the request on the questionnaire for any further experiences as a mature-age student. Nearly half of the respondents had something to say about husbands and/or children. For some, there was the gratefulness of being allowed to take time out for study:

★ An understanding spouse is a boon. While my husband is not interested in my school work, he is tolerant of me and the time that I need for homework. (32-year-old with three children, and studying for the HSC)

Others worked in a less tolerant atmosphere:

★ Returning to study created great strains in my marriage. My husband was unable to accept my lowering standards with regards housework, entertaining, etc. It irritated me that he regarded my studies as a 'hobby' which could be set aside at a moment's notice. (37-year-old with two children; had studied HSC, then psychology, divorced)

In the interviews, 38 of the 46 women spoke of their husbands', ex-husbands' or partners' attitudes to their study, although only 31 were in a marriage or long-term relationship at the time. Four were either single or widowed, and eleven were separated or divorced. (See Table 7 in the Appendix for marital status of the women in my sample.) Bearing in mind that self-image is commonly related to the way in which others see us, I have tried to categorise reponses in a way which indicates the varying attitudes of husbands and partners that women experience when they return to study.

Sally's husband was actively supportive:

★ I meet him on a good intellectual level. He would go batty if I told him about the number of bubbles I made in the dishwater.

Sally, aged 36, who was studying for an honours arts degree, was married to a senior public servant with a PhD. Her comment illustrates the type of intellectual relationship some of the couples in this category share.

Eleven of the 38 interviewees said that their husbands or partners were actively supportive in that they not only agreed with the principle of their renewed learning, but also shared household chores, either by taking the children away at weekends to allow for essay-writing or reading, or by cooking meals, or both. It seemed to me when checking the education and occupation of each of these eleven husbands that there might be some correlation between their own job status and their attitudes to their wives. Six of them were in upper professional or professional occupations, and five had tertiary qualifications higher than those to which their wives were aspiring. It is my contention, though I cannot prove it here, that the unequivocal acceptance of the educational paths of their wives hinged on the fact that these husbands were in no way threatened because they were in a high earning bracket and their wives were working towards a degree that did not challenge their own educational attainments. Three of the women whose husbands were in upper professional or professional occupations were definitely working towards careers, and three were studying for intrinsic reward.

Of the remaining five who received active support, two, aged 32 and 36, had no children, and had negotiated shared household and financial responsibilities earlier in their marriages. Their husbands in each case were skilled technicians with diploma-level qualifications. One of these women had deliberately chosen a career path, while the other was unsure depending on whether or not she was able to have children.

One women, the wife of a bank officer with no formal tertiary qualifications, saw her husband's support as the direct result of his expectations of a large pay packet when she was eventually employed. Another, whose husband was a clergyman and committed to community work, was grateful that his wife was so happy and fulfilled. She had studied at a women's learning centre and had been part of its administration. The remaining inter-viewee in this category, whose husband was an accountant, arrived at a situation where her husband's support was freely given after much discussion and negotiation. He took joint responsibility for such household chores as collecting and sorting washing and buying food and clothing. This is different from helping with housework because that suggests that the woman bears the ultimate responsibility for the household. She claimed that it was only through the type of learning environment she had experienced that she was able to come to this understanding with her husband. The shared experiences, support and learning processes at the women's learning centre she attended had combined to free her of any guilt, and provide her with the confidence to renegotiate the expectations she and her husband had of marriage.

As for the acceptance of study as a legitimate use of a wife's time, a study based on research conducted in France found that the most frequent contribution of wives to the 'social capital' of the marriage was social respectability. This is an interesting finding in view of the numbers of women in my research who did not have career aspirations. It may account for the tacit support and tolerance received by four of the interviewees from their husbands. Returning to the eleven who received active support, these French findings throw some light on the perceived benefit to spouses in what is termed 'cultural capital':

★ Cultural capital can be measured either by the educational diplomas held by the wives, which could be turned into economic capital by taking a job, or by what the diplomas yield in terms of general or feminine cultural assets, or by the contribution made by activities such as reading, interest in art etc. to the 'culture generale' of the couple.

Marceau added that most wives held 'feminine' diplomas, giving access to service careers deemed appropriate to the female roles of the upper middle classes. Only one of the women in my study who had active support from their husbands aspired to what might be considered a non-traditional career in accounting.

Active support can be seen to have been most freely offered by highly qualified professional men. In fact, the 'active support' category accounts for all but two of the professional men who were husbands of the interviewees. Those women who saw themselves in a position to negotiate, either by virtue of few household responsibilities and no children, or because their educational experiences had equipped them to discuss their situations rationally with their husbands (two in each case), illustrate a significant difference in approach from those who clouded their enjoyment of study with a pervasive sense of guilt.

Token support or tolerance of their adult education was reported by four interviewees. Three of these women said that their husbands were a little threatened by their new 'cleverness', but had become resigned to it. The other, Pamela, a science undergraduate, aged 39, whose husband had a professional qualification, attributed the passive nature of his support to the fact that she had never actually asked him to help. She said, 'Only recently I realised that if I had wanted help, I should have asked for it'. This observation of Pamela's shows how we often accept the traditional roles of men and women without thinking very much about how they apply when we move away from what is expected of us as women. Comments such as the following illustrate the attitudes under which seven of the interviewees studied: 'It might not get you a job or a big career, but it's amusing you.' That particular husband was a skilled technician who scoffed at his wife's interest in the humanities as he considered maths and sciences, the areas in which he was trained, to be the only useful areas of study. The interview revealed that there were rifts in the marriage. Apathy in itself is patronising in that the activity of study is ignored as an unimportant use of time.

As active support by husbands seemed to correlate with socioeconomic status based on occupation and education, I tried to make some comparisons in this 'apathetic or patronising' category also, but the results were not as easily interpreted. For example, the wife of a doctor said that her husband was not at all concerned about her studying a fine arts course because he was quite happy as long as she was enjoying it. It was only the tone of voice in which this observation was delivered that suggested to me that there was a 'keep-the-little-woman-happy' undertone. I may be doing the doctor an injustice.

Another interviewee gathered that her husband, a skilled

technician, 'let her have her head so that she could get it out of her system'. In other words, study was seen as a hobby, 'a fun thing to do', and, as two of the interviewees in this category said, 'not to be taken seriously'. The notion that 'it was just something that you do when he was not around' was mentioned by a student from a working-class home, and confirmed by another in a similar environment.

Altogether there were five interviewees whose husbands were intolerant, two from working-class homes, and one of whom was married to a Maltese immigrant. His expectations of marriage required that the woman's priorities be centred on the home. Another husband maintained that his wife's studying was a contributing factor to their impending marriage breakdown, while the separated husband of another woman definitely blamed his wife's return to study for their separation.

The subject of marriage breakdown is discussed in more detail in chapter 4, but it is interesting to note here that five of the twelve divorced or separated interviewees spoke of the intolerance of their ex-husbands regarding their return to study. In three cases they deferred to their husbands' wishes, only returning to study after separation or divorce. A number of interviewees commented on the women who had dropped out of classes because of pressure imposed by husbands who were intolerant of their new educational interests.

There were eight interviewees who had or had had their study activities disparaged by their husbands, or ex-husbands. One who was divorced claimed that she would not have been allowed to study when she was married, and a similar sense of possession of her time was expressed by Rosemary.

★ Everyday was his day and what I did depended on his movements. Since he's left, every day is my day. A lot of women find themselves when they are alone.

Four of the eight women who had their efforts belittled by their partners live in working-class homes, one being married to a Greek immigrant. Two were divorced and the occupations of the husbands of the remaining two were skilled technician and clerk.

In the 'actively antagonistic' category, the story of Marion, a young mother of 34 with three children, was the most poignant I heard in my entire research. Almost by chance, she became interested in HSC subjects being offered at a local women's learning centre. She described her situation:

★ My husband was happy with day classes but when I started bringing friends home from the Co-operative and started studying at home, he didn't like that. While it didn't interfere with his life, he didn't mind, so I worked when he wasn't there. He became very domineering and didn't want me to study at home at all.

He resorted to locking her in the house and forbidding her to use the telephone. When she did seek help by telephone after two weeks, he found out and had the telephone disconnected. She had no transport and he discontinued the housekeeping money. She left her husband for a short time, but was reconciled for financial reasons and for the sake of the children. When I spoke with her, she has refused a place in a tertiary institution because she did not have the energy to fight any more. Her self-image was obviously very low as her reflection indicated:

★ He feels cheated and I feel cheated. He thinks he should work for his wife and children and in return, I should give him myself, which has really defeated me. I feel I have lost myself for the sake of my husband. I really feel like a small person.

Marion's husband's occupation was relatively unskilled, but he was ambitious and steeped in the idea that he should be the breadwinner caring for a dependent wife and children. Betty, a working-class student aged 34 who worked in a factory, faced a more passive resistance from her husband:

★ As soon as I want to do something for myself, he won't help at all. In fact, he does all he can to stop me from studying.

Again, a class analysis does not necessarily fit the data in the 'actively antagonistic' category. For example, a retired middle-class man turned the radio on when he saw that his wife was studying and was antagonistic in a number of small, irritating ways which disturbed her concentration. He was also extremely antagonistic towards her belated education in front of their friends.

To sum up, if the positive categories 'supportive' and 'tolerant' were grouped together, only fifteen of the 38 interviewees studied in an atmosphere of encouragement or acceptance. The other 23 coped with varying degrees of negativeness which no doubt detracted from the confidence with which they approached the task of studying.

Most of the husbands in the upper occupational categories offered support or tolerance. Those who were patronising or intolerant were from all occupational levels, mostly from skilled areas, while those in the remaining negative categories were mainly from the middle to lower occupational levels. It can be seen that, although attitudes of husbands or partners show some variation along class lines, the pervasiveness of patriarchal attitudes in all but the most supportive husbands suggest that the problem of support or otherwise in the home still rests on attitudes to women's roles which are prevalent in society as a whole.

Some of the attitudes displayed by husbands and related to me on the questionnaire did not fall into the above categories, but I have included a selection in order to illustrate the point that in many cases attitudes to the role of women have not changed significantly from the generation of the father to that of the husband. In this sense, many of the constraints on the development of a sense of self which many women experienced in earlier schooling are still in existence in their maturity.

★ My husband left school at thirteen. He was not interested in education and believed that I should stay home and firstly look after him, although working would probably have been acceptable because of the money, so long as I could manage the housework as well. I doubt if I could have coped with study if we had stayed together, even though I probably have as much to do around the house as before. The work is not the problem, but the pressures put upon a person. (42-year-old divorcee, studying for the HSC)

★ I find is almost *embarrassing* to study when my husband is at home—he doesn't scoff, exactly, but I feel he would prefer me to put his priorities first. (42-year-old, studying for the HSC) [her emphasis]

★ I don't have an understanding husband, so he doesn't help me very much, as he cannot understand my need to go back to school when I wouldn't necessarily be achieving any qualifications. He would have preferred me to play sport or to do pottery.

One mother of five, who returned to study after nineteen years to update her qualifications, was so worried about her husband's reaction that she did not tell him for a month. When she was qualified and working again she managed to avoid telling him for six months because she felt it would have been 'traumatic' for him as he believed that husbands should be the ones to provide for families.

Even when the women who return to study are not married, long-held attitudes to traditional roles can affect the way others view their action. A friend who left school at sixteen has recently completed a BA with honours. Her brother effectively reduced some of her pride in achievement by making the observation that it must have been easy for her because she had no children. The fact that she had left her paid work and chosen to make a full-time commitment to studying so that she would feel more confident in her job where most of her contemporaries had degrees was not enough to earn his encouragement.

Attitudes of friends

The furtive adult student does not hide her actions only from her family. Reactions of friends often produce feelings of guilt and awkwardness leading to a silence about other-than-home activities. Many of the questionnaire respondents commented on negative reactions from friends, and their method of dealing with criticism was invariably to refrain from talking about their return to study. Twenty of them said that their friends tolerated their study, six had supportive friends and twenty had apathetic or antagonistic reactions from those they considered friends. A 38-year-old evening student at a suburban high school offered a comment on the questionnaire which illustrated both the attitudes of those women who were studying and their antagonists:

★ I have lost a couple [of friends] along the way. They seem to be threatened by my new direction in life. I have always, even from the very start, been careful not to flaunt my newfound knowledge.

However, any conversation pertaining to my studies is avoided.

An arts student in her late thirties said that she suffered lack of acceptance and even downright derision from friends and members of her local community. A slightly older woman noticed that her friends generally chose to ignore the subject of her studying, but to the one or two who did enquire why she bothered to do it, she replied, 'Why do you play tennis?'. She said that it was terribly hard to explain to those who had not been bitten by the 'learning bug'. Another woman, aged 32, with three children, expressed slight resentment at the attitudes of friends and relatives:

★ I have felt myself pressured into trying to justify my interest in returning to study to my friends and relatives. The fact that I am revelling in it does not seem a valid reason to them. Attending evening classes with adults who share a similar feeling as I, has helped.

The antipathy of friends has been explained as a 'backlash movement' when women struggle to maintain the old order. Even slight changes in roles, for example, becoming a student, are threatening to some of those who do not participate. Because housework has no effective measuring rod for efficiency, the implication when some women add an extra role, such as work or study, is that the non-participant is lazy or inefficient, and hence those maintaining traditional roles often react against women who pursue additional roles.

A 43-year-old divorcee was quite pessimistic about the effects of her returning to study, altough she had greatly improved her position in the workforce. I feel she tended to blame herself alone for creating the tensions that her return produced:

★ It has contibuted to the dissolution of my marriage and has put a barrier between myself and others who feel threatened. For this reason I never mention having a degree in social settings. It has created pressure on my children to strive for either equal or better qualifications, has put me in a minority group as most of my long-term frineds, and the social stratum from which I originated, do not have the same educational values. This sometimes leads to an identity crisis as I was brought up working-class (with some middle-class values thrown in) and don't always feel comfortable in either situation.

Ways of dealing with disapproval of friends

★ They don't know that another world exists—it's either don't talk about study or be called a smart-arse.

Laura, whose sentiments these are, was an arts student at university. She did not talk about her studies with friends, but 'slipped back into talking about babies and cooking'.

Interviewees had various methods of dealing with the implicit or explicit disapproval of friends. These were interesting in revealing the view of the adult student herself about the legitimacy of her actions. Seven women simply did not speak about study because they did not want confrontation, did not want to change anything, or did not want to hurt anyone. One woman felt the need to justify her returning to study to her friends and two felt that their friends saw them as selfish people. Five women explained the apathy or reaction of their friends in terms of their being threatened, and suggested that returning to the workforce would not have constituted such a threat. Three of the interviewees sensed that their friends were jealous of what they were doing and two kept token engagements with old friends although they found them boring. At least these ten women who saw a fault in their friends' perceptions were more positive about the legitimacy of their own actions than those who chose not to speak about it at all.

Caroline, aged 43, and studying for a BA, having completed the HSC at a high-school evening class, had accepted her dual roles of mother and student, and also the fact that she had different types of converstaions with those who met her in either of those roles.

★ Before I felt it hard to talk 'Mum' talk; now I can drop into it because I know I can get out into my other world. It's not that feeling of , 'Oh, my God, I'm drowning, I'm being swallowed up in all this'.

This was her reaction to comments from her friends such as, 'Oh, well, I guess I don't speak to you for the next few months'. The family doctor, treated as a friend by the interviewee, remarked, 'You really ought to let your husband wear the pants'.

Heather, aged 41, preparing for the HSC, felt that her friends were always thinking, 'Why is she doing it?' Her reaction was to be aware that she might be boring at dinner parties where she might be tempted to 'launch into an argument'. Ann, aged 53, studying for the HSC and from a working-class background, did not talk about her study because she did not want to hurt anyone. This very gentle woman could sense the feeling of inadequacy that her action might create in her friends. Betty, aged 32, also studying for the HSC and living in a working-class environment, found that some of her friends did not want to continue the friendship when she began studying, but she didn't mind because she no longer had much spare time.

There were no recurring factors, such as age, socioeconomic position, place of learning or marital status, in the backgrounds of the women who mentioned such attitudes which might have accounted for their varying responses to the attitudes for their friends.

Formation of new friendships

Friendships based on common interests fostered by study were reported by many women. Discussing such friendships, one student said that all her friends were now women at university, whereas previously she had relied on the wives of her husband's friends for social contact. While discussion of subject matter and intellectual stimulation were important bases for the development of friendships, there was another element, which was illustrated in the following comment on the questionnaire completed by an evening-class student at a suburban technical high school:

★ I have made some new friends with girls (all mature-age students) approximately in my age range, 35 to 40, all with the same goals in mind, and we give each other encouragement and the will to carry on, as combining part-time study and a family is quite a task. Sometimes when an essay doesn't receive the mark we were hoping for, we can

become demoralised and begin to wonder if it is really worthwhile, when we could be enjoying ourselves, shopping or entertaining [lunching at friends' places] but when you do well and receive a pat on the back, it all seems worthwhile.
The comment was similar to another from a student at a suburban high-school evening class who said that she had made close friends with two other older women students, because they all felt very isolated and needed to help each other.

The other element is the sharing of experiences relating to the common goal of getting credit from the teacher as well as credentials from the educational establishment, both of which are means of improving self-esteem. Again, I point to the paradox in this situation. In a competitive environment, while a degree of solidarity and support is often required between people who are in the same situation of trying to achieve against difficult odds, it is the individual who is competing for marks and credentials against all others. This 'ideology of individualism' in adult education has been noted in Great Britain also, with the conclusion that the commitment of adult education to reach a wider population will continue to be misplaced if the commitment to meeting individual need is understood and given a context only within the cultural bias of the individualistic and competitive standards. Surely in an environment where adults freely choose to return to study there is room for the development of a more critical understanding of social values which shape our expectation of education, as well as those which place constraints upon the individual.

I have found that friendships *do* grow even when there is a need to reach certain academic standards, but it seems that there is a particular type of learning environment and teaching method which encourages this. Discussion and analysis of subject matter, whether in the perception of examination material or in less formal classes, can create bonds and improve self-image when the atmosphere is supportive and unthreatening. A 38-year-old student at a women's learning centre had this to say:

★ Although I was not successful in passing English expression, my year at the Co-op was most informative and satisfying. I made many friends, shared problems of study, home, children, husbands and still came out of the year feeling a better person for the experience. This year I have attempted a further HSC subject [human development and society]. This time I feel more confident about approaching an exam situation (a major hurdle in the past) and am enjoying the challenge of study once more.

The teaching methods and the ability of the teacher to facilitate discussion is an important consideration, as I have suggested in the previous chapter, but even more so is the philosophy of the learning establishment. If it primarily emphasises the gaining of credentials, time will not allow for discussion which might be rewarding for the group even if it falls outside the immediate issue at hand. If the opposite applies, and a personal experience is aired and valued for its contribution to a wider understanding of the issue, friendships are formed on grounds considerably wider and deeper than the sharing or credential-seeking goals and their associated problems.

Eleven of the interviewees specifically mentioned friendships based on sharing of life experiences; nine of them were attending, or had attended, women's learning centres. Five of the nine who were at the time at tertiary institutions kept close ties with the centres. The remaining two interviewees attended high-school evening classes, and each remarked on the ability of the teacher to foster group discussion and even group activities outside the class time.

I have no doubt that many women have found friendship and affirmation in classes where the emphasis is on preparation for formal examination, despite the competitive nature of such an environment. But, the very nature of these classes—in a classroom or other formal setting, where goals are preset by an examination system—inhibits the nurturing of friendships, very often because of the shortage of time.

A number of the interviewees had previously belonged to school mothers' clubs or book groups, or had completed a number of short courses, but indicated a need to share, at a more intellectual level, their aspirations and fears. Pamela, a science undergraduate, summed up the conflict between social expectations and her personal need, and highlighted her sense of identification with a learning environment:

★ I didn't like being a mothers' club person. I'm not very sociable that way. I like tennis and I was going to the tennis club, but I didn't belong there. I *belong* at Monash [University].

Pamela found that talking to a group of university women with children, formed for the purpose of arranging childminding and other activities, had been therapeutic and enlightening for her. In fact she said such contacts were vital to her success as a mother and a student.

★ The student Parent Association saved me. I'm old enough to have been socialised into thinking that mothers should be around all the time. That's very hard to overcome even though I know intellectually that women should be free.

Here is evidence again that discussion at a personal level with a group which shared similar experiences was an important element in Pamela's throwing off her feelings of guilt, and in developing a satisfactory self-image.

Patriarchal attitudes and perceptions of self

Many of the attitudes of husbands, children and friends can be seen to be 'patriarchal' or male-dominated, in that they incorporate assumptions about behaviour appropriate for woman's role and about appropriate use of time. Comments made during interviews and in discussions with women's learning groups further illustrate the extent to which the notions of women's roles and appropriate conduct pervade the institutions of our society, particularly marriage.

★ Husbands don't like to see a woman changing from housewifely and craft interests. I now have opinions. If I challenge him, he will say I have changed. I am not the same woman any more.

★ My husband does not like to have his ideas challenged. Now that he has a wife who can say, 'Can you show my why?', he doesn't like it.

★ My husband bought a 'little interest' for me. He gave me a chicken bar!

We can choose to accept or reject these ideas of how women should not act. The important thing is to be aware of how they affect our own view of self. In the context of education for women, these attitudes have been described as constituting a 'male hegemony', which can be defined as 'a whole series of separate "moments" through which women have come to accept a male-dominated culture, its legality, and their subordination to it and in it'. My research was concerned with details of such 'educational moments', both in the learning environment and in the home and wider community, which contributed to the experience of the woman returning to study and which helped to determine her view of self. In other words, any attitudes or actions which sought to place women in a position of subordination and which reflected the idea of femininity as being synonymous with domesticity were seen to be essentially patriarchal.

Patriarchal attitudes, sometimes expressed in actions, are not displayed by men only. They are so common in our society that many women have internalised them and use them to legitimate their own positions, or to criticise the actions of other women who move outside the boundaries prescribed by this scheme of values. I am concerned with the effects of disparagement of her educational efforts on the adult woman's view of self. She is quite capable of 'playing down' her own efforts when she feels the situation demands it, as the following unsolicited comments on the questionnaire suggest:

★ You look up to a man. It can be bad to be too successful in case men don't like it.

★ If one of the girls from university rings and I talk and talk on the telephone, I'm very aware of my husband. It can be very boring for him. I don't make it my life's work. I tend to do the opposite—I tend to play down uni. He isn't qualified. He is much more intelligent than I am. It [study] can monopolise the whole family's time.

Sometimes mothers of mature-age students also take the stance that their daughters are doing something rather suspect when they return to study. Some prefer to ignore the situation by not taking any interest whatsoever, and others fear for any changes that might occur in their daughters' marriages. 'Does your husband mind?' was the first question asked by one mother when her daughter told her of her study plans. Others, of course, are helpful and understanding.

Three women expressed a fear of being labelled 'feminist' although their comments suggested a desire for recognition of their important role as workers in the home. Another three expressed their intolerance of feminists who, in their respective opinions, either 'deny women the choice of staying home if they wish', or 'raise "hackles" because they imply they are sorry for women at home', or 'take the opportunity, when in positions of authority, to put other women down because they are not committed feminists'.

It is understandable that some women might feel less committed than others to a cause, be it feminism, environmentalism or any other social or political issue. A student from a women's learning centre argued that 'the feminist movement had done a lot of harm by creating splits betwen women'. She went on to explain that only in the discussion of life experiences at the women's learning centre did she understand how both sexes had been socialised into their roles and expectations. She claimed to be a feminist, but not a member of the feminist movement. This need to deny association with the feminist movement which I often noticed is perhaps an indication that feminism, perceived as something which is imposed upon unwilling individuals, can be just as threatening as any other 'ism'. It is certainly not my suggestion that all women accept feminism without first examining and understanding its strengths and weaknesses. It is the unquestioning acceptance or rejection of *any* 'ism' that I see as dangerous to one's personal development. The education that women, and indeed all adults with their wealth of life experiences, should seek is one that has as its most important component the questioning of assumptions underlying beliefs and values. Once questioned and discussed, the individual is free to make her own choice and she is thoroughly equipped to defend it.

FOUR
SO WHAT'S DIFFERENT?

When a great deal of time is devoted to study, it is understandable that the adult woman student has to make some adjustments to her daily life, be it in the home, the paid workforce, or both. Perhaps she has less sleep. Other family members may take a share of household responsibilities, or perhaps she has time release from work. The fact that she uses time to study indicates its importance for her and yet she might go to great lengths to ensure that very little changes in her life or in the lives of those around her. In this chapter I will trace change or lack of change that took place in the lives of the women in my sample. Some adjustments simply have to be made to fit in the extra commitment, while others are positive steps made as a result of new awareness of her identity and her potential as an individual. For example, the woman who becomes aware of the constraints under which she is living, such as the demands that some marriages make on the personal identity or her tacit acceptance of low-status jobs, will often take some action to change the situation. On the other hand, she might do nothing. She might absorb herself in her newfound interest and accept those situations which she feels she cannot or does not want to change. There are some actions, such as demanding more cooperation in the household or taking a job, which are thought to be too threatening to long-established patterns of life. Understanding the choices we have is important and our education as adults should enlighten us. Change is often painful when it is not understood.

What's become of the dinner party?

As a consequence of returning to study, many women complain of difficulty in fitting into each day the family and study commitments required of them. As mentioned previously, fourteen of the 46 interviewees studied only when their children were in bed, presumably at times when they might have watched television or relaxed in some other way. Five women specifically stated that they now watched television only rarely and twenty said that they had less social life, particularly entertaining at home. This was not always said regretfully. In fact, it was implied by two women that study had released them from socialising, an activity they saw as boring. The notion that women seek a community of interests outside the domestic sphere, and unrelated to it, was supported by a number of comments during the interviews, some of which I mentioned in the previous chapter when discussing the formation of new friendships.

The most frequent changes that interviewees noted in the patterns of their lives did not relate to household tasks or entertaining, but to those activities they saw as personal. They commented that they had given up things they liked to do, such as reading newspapers, novels, or any reading unrelated to their courses. Buying things for the home had been postponed by two interviewees until they had finished their courses.

Home responsibilities

★ I could ask for help if I went to work, perhaps, but with study, it's different.

This comment from a member of a discussion group at a women's learning centre indicates perceived priorities both in the mature-age woman herself and in her social circle. Study is not important enough to warrant asking for help with household duties, presumably because it is unpaid. So is housework. It follows that one does not ask a paid worker to help with unpaid work because his or her time is more valuable. No wonder so many women choose to join the workforce and to study for that end. It is a matter of proving that one's time on this planet is as valuable as anyone else's. In a period of rapid change in technology and the labour market, particularly with reference to unemployment and early retirement, however, it may be that *everyone* will need to reassess the value of their efforts. The earning of money will not be the only criterion on which to base a person's contribution to society.

Only two women in my research (one responded to the questionnaire only and the other also volunteered to be interviewed) had actually made the decision to reject prime responsibility for the management of the home. For one, this decision had led directly to the breakdown of her marriage as her husband could not accept her need to study, first Year 11 maths and physics, then for the HSC—all at high-school evening classes. She had very clearly in mind that she wanted a career in clinical psychology. Neither could he accept that she refused *total* responsibility for the home and children.

The other woman, Moira, who at the time of the interview was studying for an arts degree, had had a variety of formal educational experiences before studying at a local women's learning centre. She had renegotiated roles with her husband to the stage where she no longer bought household items, such as a washing machine or a lounge suite, had holidays on her own when she wished, and shared the household chores with him.

I have already discussed the eleven 'actively supportive' husbands who were prepared to help with meal preparation and care of children. This type of help has been categorised as 'dependent labour' in a test of two conflicting arguments on the sexual division of household labour. In this situation, the woman remains the organiser, the one responsible, while the husband 'helps'. Contrasting with the notion of dependent labour is that of an adaptive partnership, where the husband is sensitive to the cumulative demands of the household, taking initiatives in organising and planning. In only one instance in this study was there evidence of a complete renegotiation. Moira, whom I mentioned above, had no sense of her husband 'helping' her in the house. They shared decision-making, care of the children, leisure and work.

This arrangement is not the norm. A recent Australian study shows that women in Australia are still seen to be the ones primarily responsible for housework. However, seven of the 46 interviewees said that they had found their way around this problem by simply paying less attention to household chores and meal preparation.

The extent to which mature-age students go to maintain the household as if they were not studying has been discussed in the context of feeling of guilt and role conflict, as well as in the section on priorities of time use during the care-giving stage. The need to 'bend over backwards' to maintain equilibrium in the home environment is very strong. A very comical picture comes to the mind if one cares to think about it but it is not funny when one considers the implication for the development of autonomy of thought, improved self-image and sense of personal identity. The pervading indications in my research are that most mature-age students continue to accept primary and sometimes sole responsibility for home tasks.

Effects and influences on children

I found that comments from mothers about their study and its possible effects on their children fell into three broad categories, although these are not mutually exclusive.

1 It was considered that newly acquired study skills and their experience of study were useful for giving practical help to children, as well as providing an understanding of the demands that are made on the younger generation. Related to these practical aspects was an expected increased empathy between mother and children.
2 They felt they were providing role models which would

subconsciously influence their children's perceptions of study.

3 They discussed, or intended to discuss with them, their children's career prospects, and what they, as adults, have learned about social structures, values and pressures in an endeavour to broaden their children's perceptions of life chances.

1. *Experience of study as practical help.* The following comments are a selection from the questionnaires and from interviewees which support this perception of the link between the adult and child.

★ I will not allow my daughter to think that study is just a fill-in until marriage. I have encouraged my children to be different from me. (Lena, 44, three children)

★ I would want my children to go on to tertiary education. I think it is still broadly accepted that the only thing for a girl to do is go into an office and work. (Elanor, 32, ex-secretary, now student, no children)

★ For my daughters I want them to be married for five to ten years, have children, then are return to study. One daughter only just copes socially and with school. I want her to find a good man and to be protected because she hasn't got what it takes—she's like her mother. (Lorna, 37, divorced, three children)

★ Hopefully it will help my children—just living with a person who is very aware of things. I have more knowledge and am more tolerant. I must be a better mother. (Rosemary, two teenage children)

It is significant in these comments that there is an implicit or explicit disparagement of the experience and even the ability of the person herself. While these women see the importance of broadening the expectations of their children, particularly girls, they have not reached a stage in their own development where they can question the underlying assumptions that have formed their present view of themselves. If they had, they would be less likely to belittle their own positions as if they were entirely at fault, or lacking in certain personal qualities.

2. *Role models.* As a result of their own experience, some women are aware that they present role models to their children. Belinda, who was studying for an arts degree at a TAFE college,

said that she tried to be a role model for her girls, and that she would like them to do tertiary studies before getting married. Sarah, who had had considerable difficulty in getting through her first year accounting because of previously low maths levels as well as disparagement of her efforts by a male teacher, took a very pragmatic view of the effects of her study on her daughter:

★ I will choose a single-sex school for her which favours maths. To avoid the conflict between being a mother and giving advice about careers, the best thing I can do is to be out there working. As a successful accountant I will be a role model for my daughter.

I have mentioned the Greek woman at a women's learning centre who was quite specific about her reasons for studying and the effects she hoped for:

★ I am studying to encourage my children who are now adult men to go back to school. If I, their mother, can do it, they can. I am still hoping it will work.

There is an implied belittling of self in this last comment that suggests that this student will never see herself in a more positive light, and that neither will her sons. She underestimates her own abilities in order to shame them into furthering their education. Pamela, who was studying for a degree in science, observed:

★ You bring home books. They see you struggling with your homework like they are struggling with theirs and there is some sympathy.

But Peg's observations suggest a negative effect, if any at all, on her two daughters:

★ I wonder whether seeing the agony I am going through in meeting deadlines and writing essays will be a deterrent. They [the children] don't see me working much. When they are doing their homework, they need my attention.

It is interesting that the role of mother was rarely specifically mentioned in these comments, but rather the atmosphere in the home provided by an adult studying, books being read and essays being written. In this way the adult woman student continues to see herself as providing a setting for others, *as well as* achieving something for herself. The conflict of her own needs and those of her family is rarely discussed with the children. Rather, a compromise or amelioratory position is reached of which they are generally unaware. In this sense, the positive actions of the mother in pursuing her own needs may not necessarily affect the future choices of her children until such time as they face an event in their our lives to which they have to respond. Even then, the influence would depend on many other factors in the child's experience on the way to adulthood. The mother's changed conduct, however, in returning to study may constitute a breaking down of the perceived distances within the social hierarchy, for example between the domestic role and roles outside the family, allowing the next generation to transform its own expectations and practices more easily.

A study of changes in sex differentiation of family roles found that children from families where servicing tasks were performed by fathers were much more likely to expect that both husband and wife would perform them in the future. There could be a parallel here in that where 'study tasks' are being performed by mothers, an expectation about the legitimacy of such action could arise in the next generation. The mother's involvement in an activity outside the home, and one which is accorded status in its own right in our society, could lead to a broadening of the children's notions of women's roles.

It could be argued that going out to work would have the same effect. But married women mainly work part-time and in the sales and clerical occupations, activities to which little status is accorded. On the other hand, being a student, and in particular gaining credentials, provides a measure of legitimacy and status with which the activity outside the home is associated. I have pointed out what I consider to be the limitations of the view that gaining credentials *automatically* brings an improvement in self-image and the way others treat us, but I realise that education is an important measure of status in our society.

It would require a study focusing on the children of women who return to study to test the effect of their actions from one generation to the next. There is the added aspect in my study that some of the adults are specifically concerned to influence their children, through their actions and their advice, to reject certain social expectations and to continue education to tertiary level. It could be postulated that such actions will at least alert the next generation to challenge prescribed roles and careers, particularly for women.

3. *Discussing with children.* This positive attempt to influence children by reasoning and explaining is best illustrated by excerpts from interviews:

★ I want to teach my children about choices in life and about equality of the sexes. My daughter wants to be a physical education teacher, so I tell her how important it is to study maths. (Marion, three chidren)

For Marion, the defeat of having to defer entry to a tertiary institution and suffer physical violence from her husband because of her desire to continue studying was poignantly revealed in her attempts to educate her children. Her daughter's response to her advice was,

★ I don't like maths. I'll be someone like you who stays home and does nothing.

Jenny, a single mother, said she intended to teach her son about injustices suffered by women, while Sarah said she will encourage her daughter, if she is happy and well adjusted, to study in a non-traditional area. She wants her children to do tertiary education, not necessarily as a 'meal ticket', but because she considers it opens up a whole span of activities and knowledge from which she does not want them cut off.

There are a number of points to be made about changes, both personal and in the perception of children about the roles of women. If the woman's role as primary care-giver with the connotations of little personal autonomy is not challenged, there can be little change in perceptions of the responsibilities of each sex. In addition, if the mother offers help and understanding with her children's studies, this serves to reinforce her 'nurturing role', particularly if she makes it clear that her study does not challenge the established priority of her time use, that is, if she makes a point of placing family responsibilities first. On the other hand, if the adult student recognises that she has the opportunity to establish an atmosphere in the home where empathy and encouragement are reciprocal, change could occur, albeit subtle, in the models mothers offer their children.

Where children see the mother in places of learning outside the home, they may be alerted not only to the possibility of entering these places themselves but to the fact that the mother functions effectively in another domain. The home-centered temporal constraints which many women suffer are challenged. A number of interviewees mentioned that they took their children to libraries and to open days at the university or other places of learning in order to introduce them to the environment in which they study, and to familiarise them with these places of higher learning.

A recent study of 40 mature-age women students and their partners in Melbourne found that, although mothers reported spending less time with each child, their children received more and better parental contact, and that there had been qualitative improvement in the father-child relationship. Fathers were not interviewed in my study, but in the few examples where husbands were reported to be actively helpful in caring for children during the weekends, it could be assumed that social contact with fathers would be enhanced.

Compromise is the key word for most adult women students. Feelings of guilt, acceptance of prime responsibility for the family's well-being, and attempts to alleviate the conflict of roles that often ensues when they return to study have been discussed earlier. Women often try to balance these rather negative feelings by noting the constructive and healthy effects of their studying on their children. Statements such as 'I can be helpful to my children in their studies' can be a rationalisation to ameliorate the feeling of guilt associated with doing something enjoyable for oneself, but they can also be evidence of an intuitive awareness of an environment which is being created for children in the home.

When the mother's learning experience contains discussion about roles and life chances, based on her own experience, there is the possibility that the child's horizons will be expanded *because* she or he has a mother who understands many of the pressures which inhibit personal growth and will act positively to alleviate them. But this positive aspect must be weighed against the deeply internalised notion that mothers *belong* to children. The negative responses of children which contribute to feelings of guilt have been noted. It is feasible that feelings of jealousy and anger could affect the outlook of the child to the extent that she would become more conservative in her notion of a mother's role, determining *not* to be like her mother.

I repeat my claim that if the mother sees her own need for personal identity and autonomy without guilt, that is, if she is aware of the relation between her long-established world-view and the new one that is coming into focus through her learning experiences, and can rationally assess the forces at work which are influencing her analysis, she will affect a change in her view of self that will be felt by her children. Conversely, without such ability to question and analyse, the legitimacy of her own need may not be recognised, or may be ignored out of fear of change, or it may be stultified by guilt. When one's actions are not carried out in the knowledge that they are legitimate and worthy, the effects of these actions on those around us, particularly children, are confusing to say the least.

I want to control my life: effects and influences on marriage

The report of the Royal Commission on Human Relations suggested that changes in attitudes to women and changes in the way women see their lives were having an influence on marriage breakdown. Studies on mature-age students both in Australia and England confirm that when a married woman returns to study, a degree of strain in the marital relations occurs. Unless the student goes to considerable lengths to ensure that her husband is not affected in any way by her studying, a situation reported by six of the interviewees, it is obvious that some adjustment is being made. The extent and mutuality of this adjustment is difficult to assess without enlisting the views of the husband or partner. The subject has been explored as far as possible in my research using responses to the open-ended question in the questionnaire, discussions with groups at women's learning centres and data from the interviews.

As discussed earlier in the section on attitudes of husbands, the degree of tolerance and therefore of adjustment to the new situation generally relates to the occupation and education of the husband and to the degree to which he feels threatened by his wife's new interest. If the husband is in a situation where even his wife's highest aspirations will not threaten his higher status, he adjusts to and even supports her studying. Conversely, if the wife's education will mean that she is more highly educated than her husband, there is tension. An interesting piece of research conducted in a Queensland mining town pointed out that most of the uncommunicative and unhappy working-class marriages were between people where the wife was more educated than her husband. When education is *currently* taking place, it could be seen as an even more immediate and unmeasurable threat because it is ongoing, and because it takes up time which it has been shown many men assume should be spent on family or hobby interests.

Strategies. When the mature-age student is not secretive about her study, that is, if she works when her husband is in the house, and when she has a husband or partner who does feel threatened, there are several strategies which are employed to avert tension. For example, Heather consciously boosts her husband's confidence by discussing areas in which he has superior knowledge to balance what she considers to be 'her chatter about her work'. Nell feels that her husband is less threatened when he finds that she still does everything the same in the home. If the woman takes the initiative in compromising, and makes a conscious effort to balance any possible threat by conciliatory action, the marriage is less likely to remain strained.

A group at a women's learning centre discussing this problem with me had quite diverse views on this need to compromise but most considered it worthwhile if the marriage was threatened. They reported that a number of women had dropped out of classes at their centre because of the pressure on their marriages. One husband left because his wife was always studying when he came home at night. He has since returned and she has compromised by studying only one subject.

Another group from a Council of Adult Education class who meet regularly in their homes reported rather proudly that not one of the class was divorced. The comment which they offered, 'We've all remained married', illustrates an awareness of the tensions and a certain pride in resolving them. Women are generally aware of changes in themselves that are a result of their returning to study, and they usually try to placate the resentment of their husbands to this change. An astute comment by a member of another learning group summed up this recognition:

★ Simone de Beauvoir's mother was left on the shelf at 35 because her husband had had enough of her. We're doing the same thing in reverse to our husbands.

There may not be complete agreement on this point of view, but the comment does highlight the sense of self-awareness that the action of returning to study sets in motion for many women.

★ Two respondents to the questionnaire wroto of the contribution of study to the breakdown of their marriages. For one divorcee, it was a major contributory factor; for the other, it was the catalyst. Her husband resented the lowering of standards of housework, and she was irritated by his regarding her study as a hobby. Faced with the choice of staying in the marriage or continuing at university, she chose the latter, and according to her comment, 'only wishes she had done it sooner'.

The subject of marital strain was a difficult one to broach in the interviews, possibly because each person was changing, adjusting or renegotiating at the time of the interview and was tentative about her position. Interviewees were more likely to discuss the attitudes of their husbands, sometimes implying strain. However, a small number were more specific. Rose, a 32-year-old divorcee, spoke of the educational

environment in which she was involved when her marriage broke up:
★ I was encouraged to be myself at the House; to pursue further education and a career. My marriage would have broken up anyway but with much more devastating effects on the children. You learn to take responsibility for your acts. In the learning situation at the House, you are stripped of 'social paraphernalia'—confronted by social situations and you are inspired by people who are actually *doing* something.

Alison saw the discussion in a women's learning centre as a possible means of healing breaches in relationships:
★ People realise that they have rights. Many marriages are sorted out because women realise that men have rights too. You realise that this is society, not just you. He can't help being socialised either.

Dora, who is of Southern European origin and lives in a working-class environment, saw her achievements in education like 'jumping a hurdle'. She worked as a hospital domestic and was studying for the HSC at a high-school evening class so that she could become a state enrolled nurse. She had a very unsympathetic husband who did not help at all in the house, despite her full-time work, and was very scornful of her efforts to study.
★ I want to control my own life. I don't want to walk out and leave him the way he is, but if he keeps up the pressure, I will do it.
For Dora, the achievement of good marks and success in her study was enough to give her the confidence to contemplate ending her unhappy marriage. She found studying very lonely at high-school evening class, having no friends of her own age with whom to discuss her problems.

A divorcee from a working-class background spoke of her ex-husband's jealousy when she studied. She decided on divorce, knowing that she was capable of achieving well as she had passed the HSC as an adult student. It seems that academic success gives sufficient confidence for some women to move out of unsatisfactory marriages, while for others there is a need to discuss and share experiences in order to gain the confidence to act.

Marion's story has already been told in the section on attitudes of husbands. The break-up of her marriage was directly related to her return to study, and the reconciliation and her deep resentment would seem to be associated with the social constraints to which she was forced to bend. She felt that action would be possible only after her children had grown up.

One student, Elizabeth, who was separated from her husband, said that he attributed the breakdown of their marriage to her returning to study, but she felt the rift and been evident before that. For Belinda, who was having marital problems at the time of the interview, her studying was a threat to her husband's authority in the home. He argued defensively and with the intention of belittling her efforts that the humanities subjects that she was studying were useless compared with the subjects he had covered in becoming an engineer. Sally felt so strongly about her new identity which was related to her academic success that she declared she would have left home had there been any antagonism. Diane, who had been separated for twelve months when interviewed, had begun a course of study since the marriage breakdown. In her comment there is evidence of a conflict between her desire for personal identity and the constraints of her marriage:

★ It was quite simple. I had a choice. I was either myself or I was his wife.

There are usually a number of contributing factors to marriage breakdown. In this study I have examined the situation of one partner in the marriage, and only one of the possible agents of change, adult education. But there appear to be two educational factors which can contribute to marriage breakdown: the development of confidence in one's own ability to achieve academically and possibly to have a career, and the recognition of self-worth which develops through discussion and sharing of experiences and problems in an informal learning environment.

In the observations of working-class marriage in a Queensland mining town to which I referred before, it was found that women with the greatest demands for autonomy in their lives were most likely to find themselves discontented with their marriages. In my research I found two aspects of this autonomy:

one which directs the individual to choose her path *within* the boundaries prescribed by social institutions, such as marriage and the workplace, and one which stems from an understanding of these institutions. This understanding allows her to choose to stay within the traditional boundaries, of say household roles or lower-status occupations, understanding the reasons for her actions, or to move outside them.

In the first case, the degree of individual control or autonomy that a woman enjoys is linked to her acceptance of the constraints of these structures. For the person who understands where her place is in the social hierarchy as well as the reasons for her position, her ability to see clearly makes her choice more complicated. She has to consciously choose to accept or reject pressures and institutions. Sometimes understanding takes the edge off anger or sense of injustice, making action to change one's position very much more difficult.

A desire for control over one's life resulting from increased ability to understand socially inflicted constraints may contribute to marital unhappiness and possible breakdown. I believe, however, that there is an important difference here in the two types of autonomy and the methods by which they are reached. If the mature-age student has developed clarity of thought through understanding of the social forces which had shaped her previous thinking, she is in a position to reject or *accept* the institution of marriage. On the other hand, if she has developed confidence and skills and, if necessary, the credentials to move to financial independence without such an understanding, she may reject marriage as an impediment to her autonomy without realising that it is an institution in which power, once understood, can sometimes be renegotiated.

Changes in attitudes to work and the workplace

Six interviewees mentioned changes in the way they saw themselves in relation to their positions in the workplace which they attributed directly to their experience of adult education. Joan, a divorcee who worked as a seamstress and who studied for the HSC at a high-school evening class, organised industrial action to gain better conditions in her place of work. She was quite sure of the connection between study and her attitude:

★ I know it is the result of my studying. That was where it all started because I had no confidence before that. I organised the strike and was terribly worried that the others would lose their jobs. I talked to the Sydney girls and got their support. It was exciting and frightening.

Joan mentioned a particularly supportive teacher and the friendships she had made at her evening classes. Some of the class had formed a film group and enjoyed social outings together.

Liz, who was studying for a business studies degree, said of her activities as a student:

★ Even if I didn't get another promotion, I would be very glad I studied. Women need to bounce back when put down. Many women say they are not going to bother, it's not worth it. But I think it is.

Liz had no children and was fully supported in her efforts by her husband, who was considering changing the direction of his working life when she finished her course. He had in mind to spend more time at home, perhaps working part-time.

Alison, who was divorced, had studied for the HSC at a women's learning centre at first with the purpose of returning to the workforce, but she had completely changed her mind about her future. She said she now knew who she was, and did not feel the need to prove anything either by studying for examinations or by finding a job, but wanted to help at the Co-operative, and pursue her own creative interests. She spoke of the restraints on the individual that she saw in the formal education system:

★ There are so many things to do. I couldn't care less now about tertiary education. If I couldn't get a job, I'd clean houses. It doesn't matter now. I've learned so many things, how to use my hands. I don't need to have a specific sort of job. I'd like to contribute to the community but my experience with people who have done formal education in this area is that it is restrictive. It might teach the meanings of words, but you can learn the same things without restricting yourself and changing your language. That language separates you from people. My only sorrow about it is that if I want a job helping in the community with kids, for example, I must have those qualifications. It restricts me but my desire not to go ahead with that sort of education is greater than my need for work. I feel quite cynical about going into the workforce because you know jolly well that in the power structure you are always going to be at the bottom.

She had no encouragement or support at home, and attributed her understanding of the social and political forces which shape our lives to her involvement with the women's learning centre.

Carol, a student and helper at another learning centre, achieved a similar sense of self-worth and said it was now immaterial whether she worked or not, although she was then training as a library technician.

★ To finish the library technician course, I will have to get a job. I could try one, but it's not a goal. I've got all I want. I could now be in the most boring job and still be in ecstacy because I know who I am.

Three of the interviewees indicated that they had reconsidered the importance of being in the workforce in relation to other aspects of their lives. For Millie, who had been involved in learning and administration at a women's learning centre, and who had returned to university to study for a master's degree, work in the 'uninspiring' position she held at the time of the interview had led to her greater understanding of the male 'bind' where the man is expected to work regular hours for the main purpose of bringing in money. Becoming the breadwinner in her family, and liberating her husband to allow him to work part-time and to pursue his many interests, was an important motivation for Millie, who also saw the 'breadwinning' role as one with a high degree of status. Her experience at a women's learning centre and later in a postgraduate women's studies course had broadened her intelletual understanding of the institution of work in our society, and her practical experience had made this understanding personal.

Pamela, a science student, had similar views. Her husband's control of his time was an important consideration to her. They have a long-range plan where they will both work part-time. She said: 'He has so many things to do and hasn't time because he is working full-time.' Jill, who once taught and at the time of the interview was a coordinator of activities at a women's learning centre, found that having control of her own time was more important than pursuing a career where she would be obliged to work nine to five, five days a week.

Changing attitudes to the importance of full-time work for the man as well as for the woman are a significant indication of a rethinking of the work ethos and of the relative importance of men's and women's work within our particular economic system. Millie and Jill, both in their late thirties, had been involved in learning and administration at a women's learning centre, while Pamela belonged to a network of women at university with whom she shared common problems and discussion. Although the adult educational experience of these three women undoubtedly contributed to their attitudes to work, there were other factors to be considered. Each was married to a professional man who encouraged her to study, each had a high level of educational achievement before returning to study and had, by the time of the interview, completed or almost completed higher studies.

Having completed the HSC at a women's learning centre, Julie was seriously questioning why she was studying for a degree majoring in media studies, when I spoke to her. She said: 'I think I will go back to the Co-op and work there and learn more about community education.' There was a political and altruistic note in Moira's new perspective on her career:

★ At first I wanted to be a teacher but now I want something perhaps with very little pay but which is political. I want to feel I am doing something. Money can't be my reason for working. I want to help women get to a position where they don't feel it's not right if they want to do something.

Moira claimed that her experiences at the women's learning centre had opened her mind to the constraints that society places on women. Rita recognised these constraints also, but was less optimistic. At first she wanted work that would fit in with her children's school hours, so she undertook an arts degree. She studied at a college of advanced education and experienced great difficulty in arranging for her children to be cared for when she had to attend classes. Her comments on the structure of the workforce and the position of women in it confirm the dilemma many women feel. Status relates to one's place in the workforce, but women invariably rank below men in occupational status.

★ Who wants to work nine to five? I have so many exciting things I want to do. Someone else gets the profits. Most women 'buy' the male system and work within it. To try to stay outside the system, still be accredited and still have status is almost impossible.

At this stage, I would like to draw attention to differences in the *types* of changes in attitude to the workplace. One group challenged the need for full-time work for both sexes and the validity of the work ethic itself. The other questioned aspects of the work ethic, such as its relation to personal status and identity, and the structure of the workforce. There were certain shared elements within each group:

Elements shared	Type of challenge
GROUP 1	
High socioeconomic status	
Support from husband	Challenge to the control of
Support from learning group	personal time
High previous educational level	
GROUP 2	
Middle-low socioeconomic status	
Little or no support from husband	Challenge to the political
Support from learning group	structure of the workplace
Low previous educational level	

The common element in each group is the supportive learning environment. In terms of the constraints on time which society places on women, which were discussed earlier, these findings suggest that women from high socioeconomic backgrounds are confronting this problem. They share this confrontation with their husbands, however, suggesting that it is a change stimulated by experiences at the more affluent levels of society, rather than by experiences based on gender. On the other hand, while still challenging the constraints on personal time, the women from lower socioeconomic situations tend to challenge the broad political structure and the place of women within it. This could be a reflection of the combined negative influences of socioeconomic position and gender experienced by these women. Such a double burden may create a greater awareness of a need to change the nature of the workplace itself to allow them more equity.

No change in attitudes to work

Most of the interviewees did not challenge the nature of work structure or the time constraints it placed on individual development, but rather their own abilities and motives. Three said that they would do voluntary work only because they would be taking work away from the younger people, one women adding that it would be a way of 'earning the dole'. Connie and Claire saw absolutely no change in their positions as a result of study. Connie, an office worker, said.

★ I used to work in a laundry and I studied typing to get out of that. The HSC hasn't changed anything.

For Claire, there was no question of a job. She said study was 'her own thing' and she was very sorry when it came to an end, but she had never considered taking a job. She had simply set out to prove to her family that she could do an arts degree.

Age was seen as an inhibiting factor by three interviewees, the feeling being summed up by Rhonda's question:

★ Who wants a 36-year-old speech pathologist with no work experience?

A sense of personal inability or failure to be able to visualise themselves in positions other than secretaries was evident in the responses of three women, two at the HSC level, and one nearing the completion of an arts degree.

Three women gave the well-known reason for choosing teaching, that it fits in with children's hours and holidays. The tension between taking a full-time job in business hours and accepting full responsibility for her children was recognised by Sally, who had trained previously as a kindergarten director:

★ I have children to consider. I really don't want to work more than from nine to three. I couldn't cope with the guilt if I had a nine-to-five job for 48 weeks a year. I was trained in the Bowlby maternal deprivation theory in college.

She really wanted to do research work in the arts field to use the knowledge she had gained in her fine arts course. I noticed this tension in two other comments where the student said that with her new qualifications she *should* be a teacher, or that she could not see any other scope but in teaching.

The need to 'do something useful for others' was mentioned by four women and a further four were uncertain whether this help would be in a professional capacity or as an act of community involvement. Belinda questioned herself thus:

★ Do I see myself as a professional [psychologist] or do I see myself as a sort of voluntary worker who helps the community? How big an issue is money for me?

At the time of the interview, she had not answered the question. June simply wanted to help without being a professional, although she had completed a postgraduate diploma in health education.

Those who were uncertain of their prospects or their desire for professionalism, and those who chose happily or otherwise to be teachers, can be seen to be trying to accommodate their positions in the workplace into the traditional patterns of wives and mothers. I see this as transposing the private image into public life and I do not disparage it, provided there has been some reflection and analysis of this situation. Without understanding one's actions, such a compromise can often lead to tension and ambivalence in both places of work, the paid and the unpaid.

I stress the point that counselling should be an essential part of education for the adult woman, whether she initially aspires to the workplace or not. In this way, reasons why she is or is not choosing a particular career can be discussed and seen in the broader social, cultural and political context. These aspects of learning are particularly relevant to women who see conflict between their own and society's assumptions about their roles yet are unaware that their own internalised view of self and their capabilities are products of those very assumptions.

The work/study mix: upgrading qualifications

The question of the effects of study on the quality of work of those already in the workforce was not broached in my study, but a letter received from the deputy principal of a suburban primary school in response to a newspaper article I had written gave some insight into a problem which could well be the subject of further research. Mrs W. spoke of a strong sense of personal gratification and improved self-esteem when successful in upgrading qualifications, but she also mentioned a darker side. She felt she was always having to make decisions in terms of conflicting priorities. She related in point form her own experiences of attending lectures after school and fulfilling course requirements, as well as those of women on her staff who were in a similar situation (no men were studying at that time):

(a) Study, completion of assignments exams, etc. all inhibited their actual work at school as they were constantly distracted by the knowledge of work that had to be done for lecture purposes, etc.

(b) Holidays were always accompanied by the knowledge of study to be undertaken, assignments and research to be carried out, in between carrying out holiday activities and domestic chores.

(c) Most of us worried about work-load distribution within the family, e.g. 'Am I doing this to the detriment of my family?' My own husband has been extremely supportive, and would always prepare the evening meal, and come home earlier from his work, when our son came home from school. By the time most of us returned home at approximately 8 pm we were too exhausted to carry out more than the minimal amount of chores.

(d) Social interaction between study groups is usually very stimulating both for lecturers and students. Mature-age students, after initial shyness, are usually prepared to question and interact well with other members of a mixed age group.

She went on to say that she had known female teachers to give up study and forgo promotion because of concern over possible neglect of the family and problems in getting work done on time. The price, she said, 'was just too high'. In addition, some husbands felt threatened by their wives' study, and the resulting tensions made the achievements just not worthwhile. She then noted the paradox in a situation where husbands feel threatened while the majority of teachers in primary schools are female and the school is usually administered by a male principal who is fully qualified.

It has been argued that the myth of female incapacity, based on the image of the isolated woman dependent on someone else's wage and therefore shaped by someone else's consciousness, is broken by her entering the workplace. It could, however, be that 'capital itself is seizing upon the same impetus which creates a movement . . . to recompose the workforce with increasing numbers of women'. That women occupy many of the non-career jobs once occupied by men, for example, bank telling, supports this claim. The idea that women will achieve liberation through work has to be considered in light of this claim, particularly as many still fill the lower-status jobs. This argument encompasses two parts of the findings of my research:

1 that many women see study leading to return to the workplace to be a means of improving the low status they experience as housewives and/or low-status employees; and
2 that some women, as a result of their experiences, take the steps of rejecting a return to work as a means of improving their status. They choose, after due reflection, to control their own time and the direction in which they use their energies.

Perhaps those who are choosing *not* to enter the workforce, or those who are attempting to democratise it by sharing the hours and the pay packet with their partners, are coming closer to personal autonomy by challenging the underlying assumptions leading to the constraints that the work ethic as well as patriarchal assumptions, attitudes and structures impose on the individual, male or female.

In summary, we can see that there was some change in attitudes and actions regarding the place of women in the workforce, but very few mature-age students in the sample actually aspired to non-traditional occupations (see Table 1 in the Appendix). In our changing society, however, it is more important that women *and* men understand the demands and rewards of all types of work, paid and unpaid. If changes in the home and in the workplace could take place so that males and females could share the workload in both of these places of work, there would be a liberation of both sexes in that each would have a degree of control over time spent at work and in other activities. The low/high status dichotomy of unpaid and paid work would necessarily be broken down. With so many mature-age women returning to study, many men being retrenched or retiring early from their jobs and growing unemployment, the time is ripe for encouraging understanding and reflection upon this important structure in our society, the workplace.

Women and the workplace in Australia

I have discussed the workplace from the point of view of the women in my sample and now would like to draw some comparisons between the current national position of women in the workforce and the aspirations of those in my study.

The desire to return to work, or to improve their present positions in the workforce, was considered as one of the possible motivations for adult women to return to study. Forty per cent of the sample did have such an expectation, and there was a general desire for upward mobility. A recent report compiled by the Australian Bureau of Statistics confirms this upward mobility between the years 1975 and 1985. The expected occupations, however, were primarily in the traditional women's areas of teaching, librarianship, counselling or social work, findings that are in accordance with figures on distribution of occupations which are released regularly by the Department of Employment, Education and Training. For these women who have a firm vision of their future work, the act of returning to study is unlikely to change that goal, although it is feasible that education which fosters an understanding of the power relationships in the workplace might lead to a challenging of some of those relationships. Another possibility, that the desire to return to the workplace will be replaced by an altered perspective on the importance or relevance of that aim to the particular individual, is supported by some comments made by the interviewees, which I have already discussed.

According to figures published by the Department of Employment, Education and Training in 1987, 19 per cent of female employees were in professional and para-professional occcupations; 38 per cent of these were teachers and 25.3 per cent were registered nurses. In my study, of the 70 women who had definite or uncertain career goals, 27 (38.6 per cent) wanted to be, or thought they might end up as, teachers and 5.7 per cent wanted to be nurses. The discrepancy between the figures for nurses provided by the Department of Employment, Education and Training and those in this study can be explained, to some extent, by the fact that six nurses who had already trained were studying with a view to moving into teaching, social work or 'more interesting and lucrative work'.

As so many adult women become teachers after their return to study, I want to put forward an idea for the reader to consider. It has been argued that teaching as a profession is most likely to be chosen by those who value highly the school and its classi-fications and credentials. By becoming teachers they can join that particular occupational hierarchy. By this means the academic institution diverts them from aspiring to rise in other hierarchies, for example those of the business world. In other words, a desire to gain higher credentials without reflection on one's underlying motives can divert attention from other possibilities for personal development, such as becoming skilled and confident in managerial occupations. These jobs may require credentials and I do not deny the need for formal qualifications. I simply draw attention to the possibility that education in traditional areas for both men and women can mask the potential of the individual for success in other fields.

There are other elements to be considered when we are discussing women. When areas such as business administration and high technology are virtually closed to them because of their gender, and teaching seems to welcome them, it is not so much a diversion of their aspirations, but often an uncritical choice. In addition, when the prevailing assumptions about roles for women rest on the image of them as nurturers and servers, teaching is one way in which the social role can be converted into a public one without significantly changing either women's basic roles or the assumption about women's capabilities. Having chosen to be teachers, they gain a certain power associated with knowledge. In this way, teaching can ease a sense of powerlessness associated with unpaid work in the home. But women occupy comparatively few administrative positions at primary, secondary or tertiary levels. The difference between choosing to be teachers and aspiring to administrative positions could be in the view of self as primarily care-givers outside the home as well as in it.

In 1981 the Tertiary Education Commission announced that an expansion of enrolments in the technologies and business studies areas in advanced education was planned to occur concurrently with the decline in teacher education enrolments. This was because demand for such graduates remained high, and many students who would otherwise have enrolled in teacher education were expected to seek enrolment in these fields. Since the adult woman is seen by the community, and often by herself, as a stereotype unsuited to management, or to technologically complex work, it is hard to imagine how the mature-age student would make the transition from teaching to technology and business without some important additions to her experiences in the adult learning environment.

According to a comparative report on education and training

for women, the lack of change in education and training opportunties in Australia, compared with those in Canada is quite alarming. In TAFE, there has been an increase of only 1.4 per cent over five years in apprenticeship training for women and this figure includes hairdressing.

In Britain, Women's Technology Training Centres have been set up to train women in non-traditional skill areas, with 'hands-on learning' as the method of instruction. They have been initiated by local women's groups and organisations, and are all-female centres with female trainers and trainees. A similar scheme has been instituted here but it does not stem from local women's groups. Under the Commonwealth Government's Participation and Equity Program, a major Victorian institute of technology has a course where women can train in electronics, and other institutes and colleges have bridging courses where women can gain an introduction to technology.

Some of the institutional factors which inhibit women in their choices of career, such as availability of subjects, times of classes, etc. were discussed in chapter 2. To accommodate their prime responsibility for the welfare of children, there is a tendency to study part-time and to seek careers that will fit in with school hours. An Australian study into women entering higher education confirms that they often want to retain traditional family roles as well as, or in place of, careers. It also claims that women's greater social concern and desire to be of service to the community leads to enrolment in the humanities and social science courses, and goes on to say that because women choose work with people rather than things, and because they want to have a job which gives an opportunity to be helpful to others or useful to society, their expectations are more realistic, especially in seeking intrinsic rewards and personal growth. The author does not question why this is so.

That seemingly innate female characteristics actually diminish the professionalisation of the occupations involving women has also been argued. These characteristics involve deference to men, the stronger desire among women for pleasant social relations on the job, a desire to relate to people in a total, rather than in a depersonalised and fragmented way, a lower drive toward intellectual mastery, an absence of long-range ambition, a lack of occupational communities, and the compliant disposition of women. Although these observations were made in 1969, some of them are relevant to the perceived images of self held by a number of women in this study.

It seems that altruistic motives for career choices, such as desire for pleasant social relations and desire to relate to people, does lead to a devaluing of the resulting work which women undertake. The changes in banking practice is an example. Women who are prepared to work part-time and with little or no career prospects have become bank tellers, a job that was once the starting place for young men who wished to have a career in banking. An account of employment in Australian trading banks states that most women occupy clerical or telling positions and, from past experience, very few are likely ever to hold a position higher than full-time teller. The same account shows very clearly that women dominate the junior positions and men the senior ones in branch banking. It seems that when women move into a previously male work area, no matter how efficient they are, the status of that work decreases.

Stereotypical attitudes towards women in management have been found in the wider Australian community. While it is recognised that women managers are competent professionals, the male nominee for employment as managers has continued to be favoured. The community stereotype of women as deferring, unassuming and basically interested in others is often internalised by women themselves so that they project an image which does not attract a prospective commercial employer.

Do women fear success? There is an argument based on the conflict between the dominant stereotype equating competence, independence, competition and intellectual achievement with success, and the stereotype of dependent, nurturing, non-competitive femininity. It has been claimed that the attitude of male peers toward the appropriate role of women, which they apparently do not hesitate to express, appears to be a most significant factor in avoiding the motive to achieve success. This may well be so in the workforce, but when they turn to education, they tend not to be quite so influenced by males in that they do desire success. As I have shown, however, there are many attitudes to women's roles that men subscribe to in the home as well as in the workplace which serve to inhibit the wholehearted and confident approach that is a prerequisite of success in any field.

I have found that pervasive patronising attitudes in offices are an important factor motivating women to return to study so that they can move from secretary to teaching, librarianship and other professions where there is an opportunity to have control over a small domain, such as a classroom. This desire to move into other professions may also be the result of the need to escape an environment which is very similar to the domestic one. By exercising 'fatherly' authority, the office manager, or in hospitals the doctor assisted by the matron as 'mother', can be seen to extend gender relations of the family, ensuring that women remain in the caring, subordinate and less well-rewarded jobs.

Involvement or otherwise in the wider community and politics

Perhaps the most overt manifestation of a change in the way we see ourselves and the world around us is the rethinking of political affiliations which generally follows on examinations of ideologies and underlying assumptions. Part of this change concerns a questioning of the expectations we hold of those in power in the many public institutions in which we as adults have some part. Conversely, a situation which does not challenge, reaffirm, modify or negate one's political viewpoint, or one which so uses the available time that there is no longer the opportunity to think about politics or the wider community at all, can be seen to contribute by default to maintaining the individual's world-view. This is not to say that all education should necessarily change one's view of the world, but it should challenge it. Questioning our political outlook in a healthy, well-informed manner may result in a more confident acceptance of our affiliations and values.

This section explores, through the interview data, the contribution of adult education to political awarenenss or otherwise, bearing in mind that the word 'politics' has a number of connotations. For some, it is synonymous with party politics, while for others it conjures up a broader recognition of the means by which administration and government is carried out at institutional, local, state and national levels. At a personal level, it is important to consider that political systems have an effect on the individual and that people can change them.

Only 4.1 per cent of the women in my sample belonged to political organisations. Nearly 33 per cent belonged to no organisations or groups outside the home and nearly 20 per cent were members of non-political social and activity groups, such as mothers' clubs, books groups and craft organisations. Church and sporting organisations accounted for most of the remaining group membership. Thirty-nine of the 46 interviewees offered some comments on the extent of their interest in politics and decision-making in community affairs. The others were unwilling to talk about this area, or dismissed it by showing their complete lack of interest.

Thirteen women found that more knowledge and understanding of political systems gave them the confidence to express opinions. Ten of these thirteen adult students were, or had been, studying politics as a subject. Beatrice became quite excited when she recalled that she had moved from a position where she did not even understand what a premiers' conference was to one where she could actually discuss events like this with others, but for Elanor her newly formed opinions were never voiced because she was 'still scared to argue verbally'. Two others also refrained from expressing opinions on current issues because this created resentment among their friends. A deeper understanding of political parties had led to a less 'one-eyed' view for Rosemary, who said she read papers avidly and understood 'that parties are made of individuals and they are not all good'. Two of the thirteen women who felt they had more knowledge of politics said that they had become more tolerant of left-wing views and particularly of union activity.

It could be argued that having a political opinion is a political act, albeit slight, but in none of these thirteen comments was there any sense in which the adult student was more than an observer of political events. Involvement at an active level was not considered.

For others, politics had some personal meaning in that they spoke of their decision to be *un*involved, and gave reasons, or they were actively involved in politics. Ten of the 46 interviewees who had previously been members of political parties, the Women's Electoral Lobby or local community bodies stressed that they no longer had time since returning to study to continue these activities.

Sally, who was completing an honours arts degree, was a member of the Australian Labor Party but had resigned. Her comments encapsulate the awareness as well as the constraints that being a mature-age student engenders:

★ There is no time. I need 'tunnel vision' to achieve my goals and therefore there is little time to see outside.

She was not unaware of the feminist and political ramification of issues such as childcare and job-sharing, as her comments suggested:

★ Until we have job-sharing and 25 hours work a week and adequate childcare, how on earth is the status quo going to change?

In a sense, Sally had avoided action by channelling her energy into her study. Collective action to redress the problems she saw would have taken time away from pursuing her own aspirations. She said that her degree would not alter her work situation as a kindergarten director, or her salary. She had to consider her children and work from nine until three.

Three women who declared their non-involvement in politics implied that they felt it a useless exercise:

★ I think a lot, but I don't get involved. I'm not into groups. (Ann, 52, HSC student)

★ I see in all organisations a lot of wasted energy. (Heather, 41, HSC student)

★ I did politics at university because it fitted in with the family. I would not have done it otherwise. (Claire, 50, BA degree)

Eleven women spoke of active involvement in some form of political organisation and saw their adult learning as a direct contribution to their involvement. Generally their interest stemmed from a recognition of social injustice, some of which had been the subject of a course of study, for example, women's health. Recognition of other areas of injustice had arisen out of shared discussion on issues such as childcare, nuclear disarmament and domestic violence. Interest in some issues developed from personal experience and in others, out of concern for global safety.

There is evidence in this group of eleven women who were actively interested in politics that some kind of personal trauma, such as divorce or death of a partner, can be the catalyst for a change in the way they see themselves in relation to society and its political structures. For others in this group, this change was the result of revelational discussion in a supportive environment where experiences were shared, analysed and discussed in their wider social context. Of the eleven interviewees who declared their active involvement in politics, four claimed that they had suffered injustices in marriage and divorce, one had become incensed by the unfairness of the bureaucratic situation which inhibited her genuine desire to be a helper in her local community, and another had completed a project on women's health services which alerted her to injustices and patriarchal attitudes in this area. Three women in this group attributed their political activity to an arousal of the recognition of social issues through discussions which arose out of shared life experiences. Different women's learning centres provided the environment in which five of this group of politically active women developed their interests in politics. Two others belonged to women's groups, one for reading and discussion and the other, the Women's Electoral Lobby. The remaining three attended formal learning institutions and had developed their interest through studying politics as a subject.

According to an account of one women's learning centre, politics can be divisive in the informal learning situation. Party politics are often seen as not something that the average woman wants to be concerned with. Combined with this reticence is the fact that few women are included in financial and political networks and it is often difficult to discover *how* decisions are made. The evidence of this study suggests that women's learning centres provide an environment where sharing of personal experiences can lead to awareness of political issues, and, in some cases, to political activity. It could be that party politics is divisive if approached as an area in itself for discussion, but when issues are first recognised, then put into their political context, the issues are made personal and action ensues. A similar fear of involvement with feminism was noted earlier, suggesting that the sequence of learning for adults must begin with an issue which can be related to one's own experience, and then move to its place in the wider context.

By contrast to those who were politically active, two interviewees introduced the notion of guilt when discussing politics. Janet, an arts student at university, aged 60, said that she did become more aware of injustices in society through the content of her study, but she had no time to join any groups. If she was not studying, she felt guilty if she was not at home. Her husband was retired. Another type of guilt associated with her high socioeconomic status which conflicted with her ideals was experienced by Caroline, a 43-year-old arts student, who said,

★ I do feel racked with guilt to the extent that I feel terribly privileged, not inhibited by practical needs. I would like to contribute back to the community. I have looked at two local community houses [women's learning centres]. I would like to have a discussion group, for example, on the poetry of Yeats. I feel for those who want their kids minded while they have a little intellectual talk. I longed for it.

Caroline's guilt contrasted with Connie's practical method of writing to members of parliament. A member of the Women's Electoral Lobby, she saw middle-class women as the ones who had to articulate for women on the factory floor who are oppressed. She felt that it was a tragedy that middle-class women were so alienated from their working-class sisters. The HSC politics lessons she had endured at a high-school evening class contributed not at all to her political behaviour. The teacher, she claimed, simply read from a book and made notes on the blackboard .

In seeking education, I contend that adult women are attempting to find a sense of personal identity, autonomy and individual status. This need arises from the tension in some marriages between the wife as part of a couple, and as an individual in her own right. In the workplace, the low status assigned to many jobs, for example, typist, produces a similar tension. From my study, however, there is some evidence to suggest that by diverting their unhappiness or discontent in this way they are very often channelling their energies away from action, whether it be political, domestic or to do with the workplace. The act of returning to study can foster an apolitical attitude, or, if interest in politics is aroused, the rigours of running a household, writing essays and studying for examination combine to ensure that there is no time to be politically active.

Why is politics a no-no?

Despite the fact that over the period 1975 to 1985 the number of women in state and federal politics has increased, there are still a number of inhibiting factors, both personal and within the structure of our society, which combine to restrain women from becoming more politically active. Fear that men will not listen to them has been claimed as one reason why more women do not stand for municipal elections. Another observer lists a number of requirements, such as resources, time, skill, experience, patronage, contacts and information, and access to networks as necessary for success in politics and adds that without these requirements women are kept at the margin of formal political systems.

It could be that the women's movement has provided a different way of organising that does not restrict political activity to the realm of the professional. In other words, it is not separated from everyday life and looking after children. On the other hand, those who are isolated in the household usually have little opportunity to develop a political consciousness. In coming together in an educational environment, it seems that women break the isolation of their individual lives and thus create a situation where a sense of political unity could be attained. As already indicated, however, women who return to study come from a variety of socioeconomic situations, attend a number of different learning venues and have diverse expectations of their learning activities, and becoming involved in politics is not usually one of these expectations.

The education of adult women will serve to perpetuate the situation where women are on the periphery of politics unless certain conditions are encouraged. First, it is obvious that the time spent in completing assignments for formal courses, together with the obligations of running a home, makes it almost impossible to find extra time for political activity. Second, when a woman takes on a course of study, she has personal goals, such as a career or self-fulfilment, which she is primarily concerned to achieve. Energies used in this way are thus diverted from issues of the wider society. There is a need to develop learning environments where adult women students are able to participate in and understand the processes of political organisation. In such an environment it is important that personal issues be related to the relevant social ones within the context of understanding our society's ideologies and structures. The decision to be active or otherwise in affairs concerning the wider community will then be a considered one, rather than one relating to the numerous and sometimes unrecognised constraints which society dictates.

I have found that mature-age students generally make few obvious changes to work done in the home. In fact, they often take pride in maintaining a situation where 'doing her own thing' will affect the family as little as possible. Some changes must occur, but if the bathroom is cleaned once a week instead of three times, it rarely upsets the lives of others in the household. In the workplace, women continue to seek traditional areas of employment where they can establish a degree of financial and personal independence, while at the same time maintaining responsibility for their families' welfare. Because time is generally very limited, it seems that women students often withdraw from activities outside the home, such as involvement in political or social groups. Even if their education does make them more aware of politics, few have time to be active in this area. The status quo is generally maintained in terms of women's use of time, almost total responsibility for children, choices of careers and generally lower status in society than the male. It is her personal time for sleep, exercise and relaxation that is most affected by the mature-age woman's return to study. However, despite the seemingly conservative nature of the exercise, most women who return to study reap rewards which boost their self-image and form friendships which satisfy the need for intellectual stimulation and sharing outside the domestic circle.

I have tried to point out the potentially limiting aspects of education as well as those which contribute to a challenging of our thinking and the making of real choices so that my readers can become more aware of them. Many new ideas are presented to us when we move back to a learning environment. They can be challenging, indeed frightening, when viewed in terms of the possibility of changes in the way we see ourselves and the ramifications of these changes in the home, the workplace and our community. As thinking people, we have a choice: we can learn *about* the past and present world as if we are observing from afar, or we can immerse ourselves in our learning so that we relate our own experiences and circumstances to those of other human beings throughout the ages. If we understand society from this personal perspective we can make considered choices about out actions in changing or maintaining our present circumstances. By now, I think my reader knows which approach I recommend.

PART III
STEPS TO YOUR GOAL

FIVE
THE BEST POSSIBLE KNOWLEDGE

The most pervasive evidence throughout my research points to both conflict and varying degrees of resolution of conflict. Two emotional pressures pull against each other, like opposing forces in a tug-of-war: the desire for improvement of self-esteem and status at home and in the workplace, and the conviction that women bear primary and sometimes sole responsibility for home and family. For some, a return to study provides an oasis, where the thirst for recognition can be quenched, albeit by dry marks and credentials. This works well, provided the woman continues to measure herself by the criteria for status that our society decrees. In this sense, she is creating a world for herself, separate from the domestic one, where she does have improved status by virtue of credentials. Sometimes there is a spin-off into the private world. Sometimes there is not.

Very often, 'finding another world' provides a means of avoiding the confrontation between the desire for a personal identity not necessarily related to the role of wife and/or mother and the social imperatives that decree what a woman's primary concerns *should* be. There is a great deal of juggling of the time and priorities in this resolution, accompanied by the chief diminisher of confidence, guilt. Even if the aim of returning to study is to enter the workforce, it is unlikely that the mature-age woman will shed this negative feeling.

The alternative resolution of the confrontation between personal desire and social expectation is easier once arrived at, but quite threatening and soul-searching in the process. It entails making a *real* choice, having recognised the nature of the two forces creating the conflict. As I have shown, some women reassess traditional education, credentials and even paid work as an adequate measure of their own worth once they realise the assumptions and values that underlie them. They have learned to challenge assumptions about their positions in the home and the paid workplace. If they have made such challenges, and positively decided to accept or reject their positions, the improvement in self-esteem comes from within, rather than from a reflection of what society predominantly sees as worthy, that is, education and/or paid occupation.

This does not mean that all women should decide *against* seeking further education and working. Certainly not! The main point I wish to make is that, by means of the education which they seek, they should acquire the skills, confidence, support and knowledge to make informed choices about their actions. If they choose to join the paid workforce, they will understand the constraints most women face: relatively lower salary, few places in administration and few networks from which to draw support. Whether they reject or accept the situation is then their personal choice.

The 'folly' of which I spoke in the introduction is now revealed. So much education can be undertaken without learning. So much energy can be expounded for reasons which are not clearly understood. Do continue to learn and to grow, but choose the path with the clear eye of one who is aware of sidetracks and undergrowth. My plea is encapsulated in Yolande Jacobi's notion of *Weltanschauung*:

★ To have a WELTANSCHAUUNG means to create a picture of the world and of oneself, to know what the world is and who I am . . . it means the best possible knowledge—a knowledge that esteems wisdom and abhors unfounded assumptions, arbitrary assertions, and didactic opinions.

Whether it be a formal credential, an improved image of yourself and more confidence or a place in the workforce—or something very private that only you realise you want from your return to study,-I suggest the following steps to maximise the benefit you will derive.

Steps to your goal

1 Find a group which is compatible in which to discuss your needs. These may be vague in your mind and only remotely to do with education.
2 Try to listen to the experiences of others and be prepared to question some of your perhaps long-held assumptions about education, the use of your time, your position in the family. An experienced teacher of adults will be very helpful in this situation.
3 Ask yourself any or all of the following questions:
   (a) Do I have a career in mind?
   (b) Do I want to help my children?
   (c) Do I see study as a means of providing something for myself or perhaps for others?
   (d) Do I need some intellectual exercise?
   (e) Am I lonely?
4 As other questions come to mind, try to be very honest with yourself, then ask yourself why you answered in that way? Try to get some idea of the assumptions and beliefs which shape your life and your actions.
5 Remember that you will be putting a strain on some relationships. Friends and family members may not always see your study as important. Try to decide where it fits into you life and how you feel about taking this time out for yourself.
6 If you decide to embark on a course of formal study, enrol in a study skills class which will give you an insight into such necessities as note-taking, essay-planning, examination techniques.
7 Don't let fear of failure daunt you (this advice comes from one of my interviewees who had battled with and very successfully overcome this fear).
8 DO NOT FEEL GUILTY!

APPENDIX

Table 1
Work aspirations in relation to present or past occupations

Present or past occupation[a]	*Expected occupation*
4 women Unstated or paid domestic	▶ Primary teacher ▶ Library technician ▶ State enrolled nurse ▶ *Respectable work*[b] *(perhaps office work)*
3 women Saleswoman Small shopowner Assistant in a pharmacy	▶ Nurse ▶ Social worker ▶ Counsellor
4 women Hairdresser	▶ Welfare worker ▶ Teacher ▶ Librarian ▶ Librarian technician
2 women Library technician Technical assistant	▶ Social worker ▶ Research worker
31 women Secretary	▶ Research assistant ▶ Administrative assistant ▶ Teacher (4) ▶ Social worker (2)

Table 1 continued

	◆ Clinical psychologist
	◆ Better secretary
	◆ *More money*
	(office or teacher)
Typist	◆ Teacher
	◆ Counsellor
Stenographer	◆ Community educator
	◆ Administrative assistant
Clerk	◆ Personnel officer
	◆ Primary teacher (2)
	◆ Social worker (3)
	◆ Counsellor
	◆ Teacher (2)
	◆ Library technician
	◆ *Better job*
	(office or teacher)
Book-keeper	◆ Research psychologist
	◆ Barrister/solicitor
Manager in Telecom	◆ *Promotion*
Accounting machinist	◆ Office worker
Bank clerk	◆ *Career to fit in with*
	family commitments
	(possibly teaching)

11 women	
Teaching aide	◆ Welfare worker
Kindergarten teacher	◆ Researcher or secondary
	teacher
Primary teacher	◆ More qualifications (3)
	◆ Librarian/teacher
	◆ Secondary teacher (3)
Secondary teacher	◆ Accountant
	◆ Tertiary teacher

8 women
State registered nurse

- Librarian/teacher
- Teacher
- Social worker
- Psychiatric nurse/
  counsellor
- Teacher of adults
- *More interesting and
  lucrative work
  (administrative or
  teaching)*

State enrolled nurse

- State registered nurse (2)

3 women
Radiologist
Town planner

- Clinical psychologist
- Community worker/co-
  ordinator

Occupational therapist (Dip.)

- Occupational therapist
  degree

1 woman
Varied occupations

- Teacher

70 women
(This total includes those who were uncertain about their workforce aspirations.)

Notes: **a** The present or past occupations have been grouped into like areas of work in an endeavour to more clearly trace the notion of mobility through education leading to work.

b Those aspirations which relate to other than specific occupations, such as more money, are italicised and indicate a desire for more respect, more economic independence and more personal interest in the work as a reason for undertaking study in order to change position in the workforce.

Table 2
Intergenerational Comparison of Educational Levels of 146 Women (%)

	Father	Mother	Husband[a]	Mature-age student[b]
Year 11 and 12	19.9	14.4	59.9	48.6
Year 9 and 10	19.1	24.6	29.0	40.5
Below Year 9	56.2	61.0	11.1	10.9
Unknown	4.8	0.0	0.0	0.0
TOTAL	100.0	100.0	100.0	100.0

Notes: **a** 114 women in the sample responded to the question relating to education level of husband. While 106 were actually married, or living in long-term relationships, 8 gave information relating to ex-husbands or husbands who had died.

b The educational level of the mature-age students is that reached before returning to study as an adult.

Table 3
Ages of children of women in sample[a]

Age of children	0-4	5-8	9-12	13-16	17-20	Over 21
Youngest	15	26	37	27	13	21
	(10.7%)	(19.0%)	(26.6%)	(19.3%)	(9.4%)	(15.0%)
Oldest	10	13	27	22	20	47
	(7.2%)	(9.4%)	(19.3%)	(15.8%)	(14.4%)	(33.9%)

a Seven women in the sample did not have children

Table 4
Age groupings of the women in the sample

Age	Number of women = 146	% of sample
25-29	4	2.7
30-34	26	17.9
35-39	34	23.4
40-44	33	22.6
45-49	24	16.4
50-54	12	8.2
55-59	6	4.1
60+	7	4.7
TOTAL	146	100.0

Table 5
Subjects studied or being studied

Subject/s	Number of women	% of sample
Sociology, psychology	33	22.6 (sociology 12.6%)
English, English literature	130	89.0
Maths, science (including biology)	26	17.8 (5% maths)
Politics	24	16.4
History	64	43.8
Human development and society	18	12.3
Women's studies	5	3.4

Table 6
Socio-economic/geographical breakdown of sample

Socioeconomic categories[a]	Number of women	% of total
1	13	8.9
2	22	15.1
3	40	27.4
4	18	12.3
5	36	24.7
6	9	6.2
7	7	4.8
8	1	0.7
TOTAL	146	100.0

Note:

a. The 1-8 scale, ranging from affluent (1) to disadvantaged (8), established by Lancaster-Jones, 1969, was used. Suburbs not included in that scale were categorised on similar criteria using the Comparative Local Statistics issued by the Melbourne and Metropolitan Board of Works, 1983.

Table 7
Marital status of sample

	Number of women	% of sample
Married	106	72.6
Separated	12	8.2
Divorced	18	12.3
Long-term relationship	1	0.7
Single	4	2.7
Widowed	5	3.4
TOTAL	146	100.0

SOURCES AND
FURTHER READING

Introduction

There are a number of theories of education and change which I
considered when formulating my research and interpreting the
data. They are to do with two main concerns of mine: why so
many women return to study and the connection between
education, particularly for adult women, and changes that occur
in their attitudes and way of life. In the last fifteen years theories
of the sociology of education tend to query, if not undermine the
assumption that education is necessarily a force for change in our
society. For example, see Basil Bernstein *Class, Codes and
Control* London: Routledge & Kegan Paul, 1974, and 'Codes,
modalities and the process of cultural reproduction' in Michael W.
Apple (ed.) *Cultural and Economic Reproduction in Education*
London: Routledge & Kegan Paul, 1982, Pierre Bourdieu *Outline
of a Theory of Practice* (trans. R. Nice) Cambridge: Cambridge
University Press, 1977; Pierre Bourdieu and Jean Claude
Passeron *Reproduction in Education, Society and Culture* Lon-
don: Sage Publications, 1977; Samuel Bowles and H. Gintis
Schooling in Capitalist America London: Routledge & Kegan
Paul, 1976 and Michael W. Apple *Cultural and Economic Repro-
duction in Education* London: Routledge & Kegan Paul, 1982 to
name a few. These theorists have been criticised on various
aspects of their work by Noel Bisseret in *Education, Class, Lan-
guage and Ideology* London: Routledge & Kegan Paul, 1979; R.W.
Connell 'On wings of history' *Arena* 55, 1980, pp. 32-55, Henry
Giroux *Ideology, Culture and the Process of Schooling* London:
Falmer Press, 1981 and others. A study conducted in England by
A.H. Halsey, A.F. Heath and J.M. Ridge, *Origins and Desti-*

nations, *Family, Class and Education in Modern Britain* Oxford: Oxford University Press, 1979, found that education did contribute to social mobility. A convincing argument to counter the criticism that Pierre Bourdieu's theory is static and allows for no personal development is posed by R.K. Harker in two articles: 'On reproduction, habitus and education' *British Journal of Sociology of Education* 5, 2, 1984, pp 117-127 and 'Bourdieu on Education' *Education Research and Perspectives* 22, 2, 1984, pp. 40-53.

How adults actually change during the process of education: Jack Mezirow 'Perspective Transformation' *Studies in Adult Education* 9, 2, 1977, pp. 153-164; *Education for Perspective Transformation: Women's Re-entry Programs in Community Colleges* New York Center for Adult Education Teachers' College: Columbia University, 1978; 'A critical theory of adult learning and education' *Adult Education* 32, 1981, pp. 3-24 and 'Critical transformation theory and the self directed learner' in S. Brookfield (ed.) *Self Directed Learning: From Theory to Practice* San Francisco: Jossey-Bass, 1985; Brian Fay 'How People Change Themselves: The Relationship between Critical Theory and its Audience' in T. Ball (ed.) *Political Theory and Praxis: New Perspectives* Minneapolis: University of Minnesota Press, 1977.

Women and girls in education: Madeleine Arnot 'Culture and Political Economy: Dual Perspectives in the Sociology of Women's Education' *Educational Analysis* 3, 1, 1981, pp 97-116; 'Male hegemony, social class and women's education' *Journal of Education* 163, 1, 1982, pp. 64-89; J. Branson and C.B Miller *Class, Sex and Education in Capitalist Society* Melbourne: Sorrett Publishing Company, 1979; E. Byrne *Women and Education* London: Tavistock , 1978; Dale Spender and Elizabeth Sarah (eds) *Learning to Lose, Sexism and Education* London, The Women's Press, 1980; Rosemary Deem *Schooling for Women's Work* London: Routledge & Kegan Paul, 1980; relevant chapters in R. Dale, G. Esland, R. Fergusson and M. MacDonald (Arnot) (eds) *Politics, Patriarchy and Practice* London: Falmer Press, 1981. Jane Thompson's books *Learning Liberation, Women's Response to Men's Education* London: Croom Helm, 1983, and (ed.) *Adult*

Education for a Change London: Hutchinson, 1980 are helpful in understanding the situation in England.

1 *Reasons—spoken and unspoken*

All figures on women in the workplace are from a quarterly publication issued by the Department of Employment and Industrial Relations (now the Department of Employment, Education and Training) Women's Bureau entitled *Women and Work, Facts and Figures* (1987).

Hierarchy of needs: Abraham Maslow *Motivation and Personality* New York: Harper & Row, 1954. Actual stages of development through which people pass: D. Levinson *The Seasons of Man's Life* New York: Knopf, 1978; E. Erikson 'Growth and Crises of the Healthy Personality' in G. Kluckhohn and H. Murray (eds) *Personality in Nature, Society and Culture* New York: Knopf, 1953. These writers take as their model the lives of men. L.L. Viney *Transitions* Sydney: Cassell Australia Ltd., 1980 and Gail Sheehy *Passages* New York: Bantam Books, 1976, take into account the relationship between men and women and the effect this has on life stages.

The relationship between occupation and status: R.A. Wild *Social Strafication in Australia* Sydney: Allen & Unwin, 1978; Ann Daniel *Power, Privilege and Prestige: Occupations in Australia* Melbourne: Longman Cheshire, 1983. Women's occupations: Joan Acker 'Women and social stratification: A case of intellectual sexism' *American Journal of Sociology* 78, 1973, pp. 936-45; L. Thurgatroyd 'Gender and occupational stratification' *Sociological Review* 30, 4, 1982, pp. 574-602. Occupation of housewife: A. Oakley *Housewife* London: Allen Lane, 1974; Kerry James 'The home: A private or a public place? Class, status and the actions of women' *Australian and New Zealand Journal of Sociology* 15, 11, 1979, pp. 36-42; E. Blumenfeld; and S. Mann 'Domestic labour and the reproduction of labour power: Towards an analysis of women, the family and class', in B. Fox (ed.) *Hidden in the Household* London: The Women's Press, 1980; A.

Daniel 'It depends on whose housewife she is: Sex, work and occupational prestige' *Australian and New Zealand Journal of Sociology* 15, 11, 1979, pp. 77-81.

Education and status of women in Australia: reports of the Royal Commission on Human Relations, Canberra: AGPS, 1977. Girls educated for marriage rather than the labour market: J. Okeley 'Privileged, schooled and finished: Boarding education for girls' in S. Ardener (ed.) *Defining Females* New York: John Wiley & Sons, 1980; Madeleine Arnot 'A cloud over co-education: An analysis of the form of transmission of class and gender relations' in M. Arnot (ed.) *Gender, Class and Education* Milton Keynes: Open University Press, 1981.

The Virginia Woolf quotes on p. 36 and on p. 124 are from a speech given to the London National Society for Women's Service, 1931, reproduced in 'Professions for Women' in *Virginia Woolf: Women and Writing* (introduction by Michelle Barrett) London: The Women's Press, 1979.

The idea that a disorienting dilemma contributes to the desire to return to study: see Jack Mezirow 'A critical theory of adult learning and education' *Adult Education* 32, 1981, pp. 3-24.

2 Meeting women's needs

Background to the provision of education for women in Melbourne: reports and newsletters from various women's learning centres and associations, e.g. Nunawading North Neighbourhood Centre *Street Talk*; J. Bremer, I. Bennett, D. Kiers and J. Laird (eds) 1980 *Plus: Community Participation and Learning* Book 3 Melbourne: Australian Association of Neighbourhood Learning Houses *A Comprehensive Report* Melbourne, 1979; annual reports of the Council of Adult Education, Melbourne—1st to 34th, 1948 to 1981.

Subjects and courses: information supplied by the Victorian Institute of Secondary Education concerning people over 25 years who entered for the HSC examinations in 1982. See also

Commonwealth Department of Education and Youth Affairs *Second Chance Secondary Education, Review of the Provision of Secondary Education, Review of the Provision of Secondary Education for Adults in the Australian Capital Territory* Report of the Committee of Review Canberra, 1985; Jenny Martin 'Women Return to Study: The experience of a group of mature-age unmatriculated students admitted to the University of New South Wales' *Research and Development Paper No. 47* Sydney: Tertiary Education Research Centre, University of New South Wales, 1977; L. Greagg, The Older Student: Occupational Choice and Academic Expectations, unpublished MEd thesis Monash University, 1974; overseas reports e.g. A. Pates and M. Good *Second Chances, 1982,* London: Great Ouse Press in association with Macmillan, 1982; P. Nashashibi 'Education for mature women: the uses of "O" level English language' *Adult Education* 52, 5, 1980 pp. 333-36; E. and E. Hutchinson *Women Returning to Learning* Cambridge: National Extension College Publications, 1986.

Women's studies: B. Able 'Resisting the tyranny: Teaching Women's Studies in secondary and adult education' *Women's Studies International Forum* 6, 3, 1983 pp. 315-18; P. de Wolfe 'Women's Studies: The contradictions for students' in D. Spender and E. Sarah (eds) *Learning to Lose, Sexism and Education* London: The Women's Press, 1980; M. Hancock 'An analysis of Women's Studies courses for adults in New Zealand' *New Zealand Journal of Educational Studies* 15, 1, 1980 pp. 54-68.

Education as a 'handmaiden of employment': A.M. Wolpe 'The Official Ideology of Education for Girls' in R. Dale, G. Esland, R. Fergusson and M. MacDonald (eds) *Politics, Patriarchy and Practice, Education and the State* London: Falmer Press, 1981.

Counselling: J.E. Gough, Distance education, mature age open entry and counselling, paper presented at conference 'Returning to Study, The Mature Age Student', University of Sydney, 1978; G. Mildred. Meeting the academic and personal needs of mature-age students in the U.K., paper presented at the same conference; E. Barrett, Access, selection and special provision for entry of mature age students into universities and CAEs, paper presented at conference 'The Phenomenon of Mature Age Students at Darling Downs Institute of Advanced Education', Toowoomba, 1981; R. McDonald and S. Knights 'The experience of adults at Murdoch University' in D.C.B. Teather (ed.) *Toward a Community University: Case Studies of Innovation and Community Service* London: Routledge & Kegan Paul, 1983. The quotes about counselling on pp. 57 and 82 are from E. and E. Hutchinson *Learning Later, Fresh Horizons in English Adult Education* London: Routledge & Kegan Paul, 1978, pp. 177 and 112.

Philosophy of informal learning environments: I. Illich *Deschooling Society* Harmondsworth: Penguin Education, 1973 and P. Freire *Pedagogy of the Oppressed* Harmondsworth: Penguin, 1972. For particular reference to adult education, see T. Lovett 'Adult education and community action' in J.L. Thompson (ed.) *Adult Education for a Change* London: Hutchinson, 1980; C. Griffin 'Social control, social policy and adult education' *International Journal of Lifelong Education* 2, 3, 1983, pp. 217-44; B. Fried *Empowerment vs. Delivery of Services* Concord: New Hampshire State Department of Education, 1980.

Relationship between education and change: A.B. Knox *Adult Development and Learning* San Francisco: Jossey-Bass, 1977; J. Blackburn (chairperson) *Ministerial Review of Postcompulsory Schooling, Report* Vol. 1, Melbourne, 1955; Mezirow 'Principals of good practice in continuing education' in *Lifelong Learning* November 1984; A. Tough 'Self-planned learning and major personal change' in M. Tight (ed.) *Education for adults* Vol. 1 *Adult learning and education* London: Croom Helm, 1983. On the way in which subject material is treated see M. Hughes and M. Kennedy 'Breaking out—Women in adult education' *Women's Studies International Forum* 6, 3, 1983, pp. 261-69; J. Anyon 'Social class and school knowledge' *Curriculum Enquiry* 11, 1, 1981, pp 3-42. The reference to curriculum as practice is from Michael Young and G. Whitty *Society, State and Schooling* London: The Falmer Press, 1977, pp. 237-42. Education as encouraging individualism rather than sharing of experiences and resources: N. Keddie 'Adult Education: an ideology of individualism' in J.L. Thompson (ed.) *Adult Education for a Change* London: Hutchinson & Co., 1980. Relationships between teachers and students: E. G. Pinderhughes 'Empowerment for our clients and for ourselves' in *Social Casework: The Journal of Contemporary Social Work* Family Service Association of America, 1983 pp. 331-38; W.W. Randle 'Reading, writing and relationships, Toward overcoming the hidden curriculum of gender, ethnicity and socioeconomic class' *Interchange* 12, 2 and 3, 1981, pp. 229-51; A. Kirajnc 'Let's do away with "toy" education for women' *Convergence* 8, 1, 1975, pp. 8-12.

Other studies on the way adults learn: Roby Kidd 'The Learning Transaction' in M. Tight (ed.) *Adult Learning and Education* Milton Keynes: Open University, 1983; M. Knowles *The Adult Learner: A Neglected Species* Houston: Gulf Publishing Co., 1973; M. Knowles Andragogy: An Emerging Technology for Adult Learning' in Tight (ed.) *Adult Learning and Education,* Milton Keynes Open University, 1983.

3 *You feel confident and you feel guilty*

Report on mature-age students in Australia on p. 108: T. Hore and L. West *Mature Age Students in Australian Higher Education* Melbourne: Higher Education and Research Unit, Monash University, Clayton, 1980.

Studies on language: P. Bourdieu and J.C. Passeron 'Introduction: Language and Pedagogical Situation' (trans. from *Rapport pedagogique et communication* Paris-La Haye Mouton, 1965, 1968) in D. McCallum and U. Ozolins (eds) *Melbourne Working Papers* Melbourne: Department of Education, University of Melbourne, 1980; M.E. Poole 'Language' in F.J. Hunt (ed.) *Socialisation in Australia* 2nd ed, Melbourne: Australian International Press, 1978. Quotation on p. 112 C. Miller and K. Swift *Words and Women: New Language in New Times* Harmondsworth: Penguin, 1977, p. 55.

Idea of 'closed horizons' and a 'means-end chain': Noel Bisseret

Education, Class, Language and Ideology: Routledge & Kegan Paul, 1979; Basil Bernstein 'Some Sociological Determinants of Perception: an Enquiry into Subcultural Differences' *British Journal of Sociology* IX, pp. 159-74. Bisseret also discusses sacrifice in terms of the way many women see their roles, a point also raised by Sung Mook Hong 'Age and Achievement: The Age Factor in Predicting Academic Success' *Australian Journal of Adult Education* 22, 3, 1982, pp. 21-28.

Observations about women feeling guilty: Elisabeth Badinter *The Myth of Motherhood* London: Souvenir Press (Education and Academic) Ltd, 1981; J. Harper and L. Richards *Mothers and Working Mothers* Penguin, 1979; B. Wearing *The Ideology of Motherhood: a study of Sydney suburban mothers* Sydney: Allen & Unwin, 1984. Bowlby maternal deprivation theory: John Bowlby *Child Care and the Growth of Love* London: Penguin, 1953. Reassesment of this theory: M. Rutter *Maternal Deprivation Reassessed* Harmondsworth: Penguin, 1972 and 'Maternal deprivation, 1972-1978, new findings, new concepts, new approaches' *Child Development* 50, 1979, pp. 183-305.

Roles as determining actions: L.L. Viney *Transitions* Sydney: Cassell Australia Ltd, 1980; T.T. Sem 'Academic values and intellectual attitudes: sex differentiation or similarity?' *Acta Sociologica* 18, 1, 1974, pp. 36-48.

The quote on p. 144 about cultural capital is from J. Marceau 'Marriage, role division and social cohesion: the case of some French upper-middle class families' in D.L. Barker and S.E. Allen, (eds) *Dependence and Exploitation in Work and Marriage* London and New York: Longman, 1982. V.L. Bullough in *The Subordinate Sex: A History of Attitudes to Women* New York: Penguin Books Inc., 1974, makes the suggestion about a 'blacklash' movement against women who choose to be successful outside the home.

Connection between the education system and the development and maintenance of hegemony: P. Bourdieu and J.C. Passeron *Reproduction in Education, Society and Culture* London: Sage Publications, 1977; M.W. Apple *Ideology and Curriculum* Boston: Routledge & Kegan Paul Ltd, 1979;

Madeleine Arnot 'Male hegemony, social class and women's education' *Journal of Education* 164, 1, 1982, pp. 64-89; M MacDonald, (M, Arnot) 'Schooling and the Reproduction of Class and Gender Relations' in R. Dale, G. Esland, R. Fergusson and M. MacDonald (eds) *Education and the State: Politics, Patriarchy and Practice* Vol. 2, London: Falmer Press, 1981.

4 *So what's different?*

Responsibility for home organisation: M. Meisner 'No exit for wives: Sexual division of labour and the cumulation of household demands' *Canadian Review of Sociology and Anthropology* 12, 1975, pp. 424-39; H. Glezer 'Changes in marriage and sex-role attitudes among young married women: 1971-1982' *Australian Family Research Conference Proceedings* Vol. 1, *Family formation structure and values,* Melbourne: Australian Institute of Family Studies, 1984. Expectations of children about home responsibilities: S. Sampson 'Socialisation into Sex Roles' in F. Hunt (ed.) *Socialisation in Australia* 2nd ed, Melbourne: Australian International Press, 1978. Many women want to maintain their primary role in the household while participating in further study: D.G. Beswick 'Why more women are entering Higher Education: The psychological conditions for increased participation' in S. D'urso, and R.A. Smith *Changes, Issues and Prospects in Australian Education* Brisbane: Queensland University Press, 1978.

Effects on children: S. Kelly 'Changing parent-child relationships: and outcome of mother returning to college' *Family Relation* 31, 1982, pp. 187-294; *The Prize and the Price* Sydney: Methuen Haynes, 1987. Changes in attitudes to marriage: Kelly op.cit. and Claire Williams *Opencut—The working class in an Australian mining town Sydney: Allen & Unwin, 1981.*

Quote on p. 180: M. Dalla Costa and S. James 'The power of women' in E. Malos (ed.) *The Politics of Housework* London: Alison & Busby Ltd., 1980, p. 180.

Teaching as a mainly female profession: P. Bordieu and J.C. Passeron *Reproduction in Education Society and Culture* London: Sage Publications, 1977; position of women in teaching and other areas of the workforce: S. Sampson 'The role of women in leadership in Australian schools' in R. Brown and L. Foster (eds) *Sociology of Education* 3rd ed, Melbourne: Macmillan, 1983; B. Cass, M. Dawson, D. Temple, S. Willis, A. Winkler *Why So Few? Women in Australian Universities* Sydney: Sydney University Press, 1983; A. Game and R. Pringle *Gender at Work* Sydney: Allen & Unwin, 1983; and *Social Report Victoria, Women* Melbourne: Australian Bureau of Statistics Victoria, 1986.

Comparative report on page 184: K. Iseman *Moving Women In: A comparative study of non-traditional education/training opportunities for women in Canada and Australia* Adelaide: Tertiary Education Authority of South Australia, 1983.

Professionalisation of occupations in which women participate: S. Macdonald and D. Lamberton 'Tradition in transition: Technological change and employment in Australian trading banks' *Australian Computer Journal* 15, 4, 1983, pp. 128-34; L.V. Still, R.C. Cameron and J.M. Jones, Women in Management: Stereotypes, myths and realities, paper presented at Sociological Association of Australia and New Zealand Conference, Melbourne, 1983; M. Grumet 'Pedagogy for Patriarchy: The feminisation of teaching' *Interchange* 12, 2 and 3, 1981, pp. 165-84.

Women fear success: M. Horner 'Toward an understanding of achievement related conflicts in women' *Journal of Social Issues* 28, 2, 1972 pp. 157-75; M. Horner, Carol C. Nadelson and Malkah T. Notman (eds) *The challenge of change: perspectives on family, work and education* New York: Plenum Press, 1983. See also G. Sassen 'Success anxiety in women: a constructivist interpretation of its source and its significance' *Harvard Educational Review* 50, 1, 1980, pp. 13-23.

Women's involvement in politics: P. Giles The hysterical politician, paper presented to ANZAS Congress, Canberra, 1984. Need for personalisation of politics: S. Rowbotham, L. Segal. H. Wainwright (eds) *Beyond the Fragments* London: Merlin Press, 1979.

5 *The best possible knowledge*

Quote on p. 198 J. Jacobi *The Way of Individuation* (trans. R.F.C. Hull) London: Hodder & Stoughton, 167, p. 129.

INDEX

Animal Tails   David Smith

David Smith is convinced that science is about having fun with ideas.

In this book he shares the fun with us. There is a contagious excitement in peptides, diving ducks, blood pressure regulation in eels and the sperm structure of marsupials as David Smith introduces us to the science and scientists of his *Animal Tails*.

How to be a Successful Student   Jill Dixon

How to be a Successful Student takes you through the steps vital to using your time and resources to best advantage. Time management, note-taking, essay writing, dealing with exams, coping with stress are all covered by an experienced counsellor and teacher. Following these strategies you'll maximise your chances of passing and still have time for your family, your friends, your recreation and your interests!

Steer Your Own Career   Dr Bob Bisdee

Have you ever dreamed about changing your job? Is your present position boring or frustrating? Are you entering the job market for the first time? Are you contemplating starting your own business? Are you thinking of re-joining the workforce?

Then do something about it!

The key to personal success is knowing how to direct your career and believing in yourself. *Steer Your Own Career* will help you do just that. The most important first step is to know exactly what *you* want from life. This book will help you assess this for yourself.

Edda's Diaries   Edda Walker

'I am determined to live until the moment of death.'

In this unusual and fascinating book we share a woman's journey – along the canals of western Europe with her family, through the crests and undertows of self-awareness; then her acceptance of life with cancer, and the ultimate rite of passage.

We come to know this remarkable woman through her diaries, her poems, her acute observations of people and places in Europe and Australia, and her compelling insights into herself.

As we come to know Edda, we come to know ourselves.

Save Me Joe Louis   Kate Jennings

'Twenty years of being a lovesick loon. Twenty years of careering through life like a horse loose in traffic. Enough is enough.'

With that realisation, Kate Jennings decides to change and in the process takes a clear-eyed and ruefully humorous look at her Riverina childhood, her years as a feminist activist, and her travels and current way of life in the United States. To make peace with herself, she sifts and sorts through subjects as diverse as school reunions and house-hunting in Connecticut, gender in Japan and Australian drinking habits, weighing her options and reconciling the contradictions.

FOR THE BEST IN PAPERBACKS, LOOK FOR THE

PENGUIN

Executive Image   Maria Bottomley

Executive Image is about the successful packaging of an important product – you.

Secretary, manager, already on the board? Rising star in the sales force or administration? You need more than talent to get on; you need to present it effectively.

Maria Bottomley's perceptive guide to appropriate behaviour in the organisation sets out the rules that will make life in the executive lane much smoother.

Retirement: Make It Easy   Gay Matthews

Gay Matthews quite unexpectedly found herself with a retired husband and, in effect, a new life.

This friendly and practical guide draws on her experiences and those of many others she has spoken to. It covers subjects from financial planning to changing personal relationships – and even hints for concocting your own inexpensive liqueurs.

Reading *Retirement: Make It Easy* is as pleasant and helpful as having a chat with an old friend.

Katherine Mansfield: The Woman and the Writer   Gill Boddy

Katherine Mansfield was not only an extraordinary writer, devoted to her work, she was also a woman of great vivacity and strength, who led a brief but fascinating life, from her birth in New Zealand to the literary circles of England and Europe. The leading writers of her age, people like Virginia Woolf and D H Lawrence were a constant part of her life.

Gillian Boddy has drawn on her years of research to introduce to us a new Katherine Mansfield, not ethereal as has been the myth, but substantial, alive.